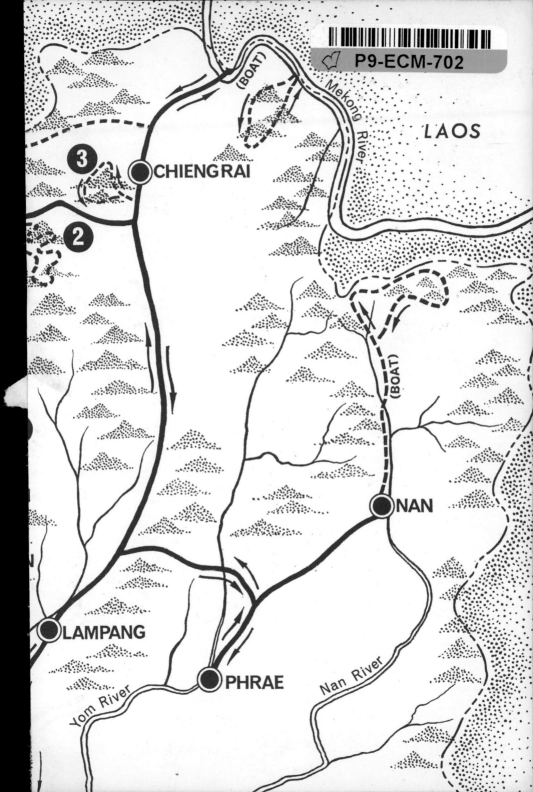

(BOAT)

Mekong River

LAOS

3

2

CHIENG RAI

(BOAT)

NAN

LAMPANG

PHRAE

Nan River

Yom River

Tracks of an Intruder

TRACKS
OF AN
INTRUDER

by Gordon Young

WINCHESTER PRESS

Library of Congress Catalog Card Number: 77-148564

ISBN: 0-87691-032-0

First American Edition

Published by Winchester Press
460 Park Avenue, New York 10022

PRINTED IN THE UNITED STATES OF AMERICA

For

MY WIFE PEGGY

and

OUR DAUGHTERS FOUR

" We hillfolks say of marks and signs, that there are two kinds—that of man and that of wild creatures. The one is but an intruder into the forest, leaving a barefoot track here and a knife-slash there. All the others, the citizens of the forest make, and more rightfully. See near the deer and the boar trails that man-sign—and you see the tracks of an intruder."

—*Chief Ca Hkaw Pheh-ya*
of the Mae Pun Lahu

Contents

Introduction

American soldiers and civilians are returning from the Vietnam War with incredible jungle adventures and stories about their unforgettable relationships with Montagnard tribesmen. For some of these individuals, the relationship became very deep, as it has been for the author of this book.

Regardless of where in Southeast Asia the particular ethnic group of mountain people are located, they share one distinction: they are among the most jungle-oriented "Children of the Forest" to be found anywhere in the world. For whatever reason the foreigner, the "Intruder" comes into this mountainous jungle setting, he will have found the going good or bad depending upon his rapport with the people of the hills. To many an American, particularly the Green Berets of the U.S. Special Forces units, the Montagnards of Vietnam became outstanding guides, companions and teachers in the bewildering depths of nearly impenetrable jungles. These were people of such different heritage and social patterns that the Vietnam conflict has taken a new and different meaning for many Americans. Here were the proud, patriot chieftains, uninterested in Saigon or Hanoi or Washington; they were concerned only with a right to live and work within their particular mountain range where virtually no other "civilized" people would care to live. They cherished the right to appease and invoke the blessings of their various Animistic Spirits rather than adopting strange and foreign religions. And in their simple, "primitive" ways, they have achieved greater morality and human integrity than more sophisticated social orders.

By 1965, the Vietnam War had begun the steep escalation that was to follow. Thousands of young Americans were destined to learn something of the environment beyond the city streets and the well-ordered state parks. Combat patrols and missions took them deep into the fastnesses of triple-canopied jungles where they imagined at first no human being could exist. It became a grim experience, made worse by many fears, founded or unfounded, of the mysterious, forbidding jungles.

The original purpose for this book was to put in print a sort of "survival manual," exposing certain truths and untruths about the Southeast Asian forests for the benefit of those who wanted to enter them or who were required to do so. The author has chosen to compile instead a series of essays portraying true adventures in Asian jungles that he has roamed since he was a boy. The theme throughout this volume is that of an American, an "Intruder," who was privileged to have associated closely enough with Montagnards—Lahu tribesmen of Northern Thailand, in this case—to have learned much about life in the jungles and among the jungle people. In this fashion, it has been possible to bring out some important facets of jungle survival, of hunting wild game, of the enchantments as well as the grim aspects of jungles, and above all of the emotions and characters of the human residents in such a setting.

This volume will have achieved its main purpose if it gives further understanding as to why many Americans speak with new fondness about a people they hardly knew to exist before their Vietnam experience. It is because of these simple, honest, brave people that many Americans have remained in Vietnam, in Laos and in Thailand for additional tours of duty. It was the predominant reason for the author's long sojourn in Southeast Asia. For it is not too far-fetched to say that we found in these hidden corners of the world people who are truly separate from the chaos and complications of more progressive societies. The Lahus of Thailand and Burma, the other Montagnards of Vietnam and Cambodia and Laos, speak different dialects but all have in common an intense devotion to their way of life and the land on which they live.

CHAPTER ONE

To Where the Trails Meet

THEY were camped by family units from just below the ridge to the stream's edge fifty yards down the steep and shaded slope. I knew immediately that they were Lahu as I stood gazing at the increasing number of men, women and children who appeared out of the forest cover.

Most of the faces were expressionless except for the wide-eyed curiosity that marked the women and children. The men, armed with fighting swords and a few muzzle-loading shotguns looked steadily at me, waiting for the lone intruding stranger to speak. None of them could have guessed that I stood before them quite unable to speak for a few moments because of the overwhelming happiness that I felt just then. I could only smile at them, thinking that twelve years had been a long time to be away, and with that last step I had completed a very long journey to return to the people of my childhood.

I had been most fortunate in running into the Lahu represented in that group, making my long-hoped-for contact much sooner than expected. These people might have been members of any of a number of different ethnic groups that lived in the mountains of northern Thailand, even among the several different Lahu tribes alone. To any but this particular group, what I was about to say would have had no meaning in Thailand. I could not be certain of that until we had exchanged introductions.

"I am the grandson of the '*Ah-pa-ku-lo*'," I said addressing the several men to my left.

"We are Lahu who journey to a new village site," a stocky man replied, showing only mild surprise that I spoke to them in their own language.

His words were immediately followed by a shout from a lean, wiry man just behind him who stepped out repeating "*Ah-pa-ku-lo?*" several times and looking intently at me. Then satisfied that twelve years might have made the apparent changes in the young boy he had once seen, he exclaimed in a loud voice: "Yo!" He threw his gun down and began shaking my hand so vigorously that I felt he might throw me completely off balance.

A pandemonium of handshaking followed after this introduction. Every one of over a hundred right hands had to be grasped, even small babies riding upon mothers' backs. Twenty minutes later, my face ached from prolonged grinning and I was sweating profusely despite the cool morning air. But I could not have been happier had I just then won the national elections.

Before the turn of the century, my grandfather, William Marcus Young, had founded a mission in north-eastern Burma. Here, my father Harold was born, and together with his brother Vincent, carried on the mission up to the Japanese invasion in 1942. By the time I made my own precarious entrance into the scene in 1927, the situation had been little changed. Within a setting of wild Wa head-hunters, warring tribes, Chinese warlords and bandits, tiger and leopard, malaria and dysentery, and the immutable natural barriers of mountains, rivers and jungle, my forebears had found the thrill of adventure and frustration of hardship at many a turn in the trail.

They learned how to survive under incredible conditions without medical supplies or modern equipment. Their triumphs were many as were their sorrows and disappointments, and in the end there were many who were enriched by their dedication to serve fellow man. Certainly, a grandson of the *Ah-pa-ku-lo* chanced later to enjoy the fruits of this labour and owes much to his forebears. I shall never forget this great helping hand that made possible the joy of finding good friends who gave me much more than I could return. So, in my turn—and quite selfishly— I could reap the many benefits of the selfless labour that had preceded me.

Though I will mention it briefly, it is my intention that a lion's share of praise be given to Ruth Saada Young, a very brave woman. I found and walked an interesting byroad in life only because she dared in the first place to go with my father to a remote little village at Bana, Yunnan, China. A thousand things she did made the difference between my return to adventure with the Lahu or an early end somewhere between birth and the first few years. On one occasion when all the men were away, she had confronted a horde of Chinese bandits bent on nothing good, and through sheer courage and kindness (treating the leader's sore tooth) she undoubtedly saved us all from disaster.

The six years before Pearl Harbour were happy ones for a young lad growing up in the Burma of those times. My father and uncle, both avid hunters and woodsmen during their spare time, taught me first how to apply my very small frame behind the kick of a shot-gun. At eight and nine years of age, I was still small for my age and to me a 12-gauge shotgun was a cannon that left me sitting happily on my bottom after each session with it. When I had stalked and killed my first deer, I felt like a hero because I could show a bruised and thorn-pricked behind, which had produced that shrill initial yell. These were battle wounds which I proudly incorporated into the repeated recountings of those moments as older hunters listened, amused and with pretended awe. Meanwhile, Lahu boys my age taught me what everybody in their tribe had to know about the jungles and of hunting, trapping, skinning and butchering. That period of childhood had but one important consideration as far as I was concerned: the correlation between the bruised behind and right shoulder and the attainment of *Hp-hteu-lo,* the master hunter in the Lahu code. These were the really necessary things in life. And so, wearing a battered sun helmet, khaki shorts, usually barefooted and with much dirt on my knees, I took to the thorny brambles with urgent zeal and joyous determination.

Lahu boys, then men showed me many a thrilling secret along the jungle trail. Some lesson was to be learned in every wooded glen we entered; something remained yet to be sought out and understood; something always eluded the hand or the eye. I learned that the magnitude of Nature's many splendours were not but a thousand secrets which could be learned in a few years. I learned that I could never lose the passion which had been instilled during those early years to return again and again to the forest; there were too many mysteries which had to be understood in order to satisfy the curiosity. Later, as a man, I found that there are other compelling reasons, some of which withstand definition. For in the stillness of the deep woods or during the encounters with some charging beast, a man might learn something about himself, and that a man, by sharing his experiences with companions, finds always a new and more meaningful happiness there.

I had not seen the Lahu since 1942 when the Japanese invasion had begun in earnest to take over Burma. From our home in Taunggyi, I had joined a walking gang to India, while my mother, sister and brother were being evacuated by air. My father had remained with British Forces and came out much later, in very poor shape from the exhausting and desperate withdrawal from Burma. My own fourteen-day hike from the Chindwin River to

Kohioma, Assam, had seemed like a merry outing to a young lad who could not yet see that the war was real at the time. Later, untold thousands of refugees followed much of the same trail on which we had walked out from Burma, many of them to die along the way in the steaming rain forests.

I took a deep breath and heaved it out audibly as I took a seat on a banana leaf by the Lahu chief's side. The events which had taken place in the past moments still seemed quite unbelievable to me. I had chanced to stumble upon the one group of hill people who, having come out from Burma some years before, had members who knew my grandfather and father. It had been my wildest hopes that remnants of my grandfather's missionary following might be found in Thailand; this had only chanced to happen as a result of the confusion following the Japanese invasion some ten years before. Out of more than a hundred thousand mountain people living in the rugged hills of northern Thailand, the first hand that I had shaken was that of Ca Va Lo, " Big Pig ", whose equal as a hunter-companion I would not find again for the duration of my stay in Thailand. In the years to follow, I walked jungle trails with many friends from a dozen or more different tribes, but Big Pig taught me more, and I shared more experiences with him, than with any other.

That had been a bright, cool morning in March 1954, only a few months after I had come to Thailand from California. Having found a comfortable little house in Chiengmai, I had ventured out into the hills to the north for a first excursion, leaving my wife Peggy and small first daughter in that charming town. By then I had cleared the " tools of my trade " through customs, consisting of a rifle, shotgun and equipment for collecting natural history specimens. It had taken months of preparation and long delays to reach Chiengmai. My first real break came when I met Big Pig and his people through, what was for me then, a blind stab into unknown mountains. This chance early meeting was like acquiring a ready-made workshop instead of taking years to build one, and certainly, it influenced my decision to remain in Chiengmai much longer than my original plans allowed.

Was all this real or had I been dreaming as I had so often found myself doing while in an entirely different world just a few months before? Gradually, old familiarities came back to me as I sat talking to the Lahu and listening to them and the sounds of the jungle around us. Here my senses began taking in again sights, sounds and smells which had been lost for years. I closed my eyes then opened them to see all around me vegetation that is not found in any park in the west. The call of birds and the din of cicadas, and the peculiar scent of exotic miniature orchids all told me that I was home again. And yet, half of the picture would have been missing if the Lahu had not been there. It was through their ways and their language that I had first been introduced to this environment. These were the people with all the answers to a thousand questions I still had concerning their world of deep forests and tall mountains. That precious key was in my hand again. My joy was indescribable.

Using a borrowed jeep while my own was still in the process of reaching Bangkok, I had struck out from Chiengmai the day before. I told my wife that I was going to " explore the country to the north of here ", adding almost as a joke that I might even chance upon some Lahu. To the best of my knowledge then, Lahu of several southern groups were to be found in northern Thailand, but no one had any information on just what subdialect groups they might belong to. As it turned out later, there were predominantly Shelleh and Nyi, with a sprinkling of Kwi, Ku-lao and the Lahu-na among whom I had lived as a boy. The most I had actually hoped for that morning when I left the jeep and the two hired men from Chiengmai, was to run into a deer or boar. As luck would have it, I had swung right into the path of my Lahu as they crossed the Mae Mao stream on their journey southwards.

I stayed there with my newly found friends all the rest of that day and night, and there had been few pauses in our conversation. At least a dozen of the older men from the north had seen me as a small boy in the days before the Japanese invasion. In the interim years, these people had moved from various locations in north-eastern Burma to Thailand, following the general trend of the migration of hill people originating in Southern China. En route to their new village, it had been voted that the entire group should stop to enjoy a few days of hunting and fishing, since the new fields had already been cut in advance and there was no urgency to reach the chosen site.

As family outings go, this was the largest affair I have ever seen. The people looked at such a major task as moving their village with the carefree abandon of pic-nickers, planning the event to include pleasure with the hard work. Each family had all of its worldly possessions, most of which were scant enough that the man of the house could pack them on his back with the baby perched on top. Women and children were responsible for driving the livestock along, these consisting of selected breeder stock and a few chickens in baskets. There were a few ponies to help with the more cumbersome community property such as the precious and essential blacksmithing tools and anvil. The journey, taken in easy stages, was four days southward along the Mak-ang-khang range.

Towards evening, I was surprised to see a number of men I had not yet met, come straggling into camp in twos and threes. I had forgotten to ask about the men who I should have known would be out hunting. They looked mag-nificent and very proud of the heavy loads they carried in makeshift bamboo baskets. These they set down at their individual lean-to huts where wives rushed out excitedly to unpack the great slabs of fresh meat. I could see that they had had a most successful day.

"Ah, the young people chose the right trail to the heh-nu today," Big Pig commented casually, shifting his position and sitting up with the pride of a successful commander.

" Heh-nu? " I almost shouted.

" Yes, I would have gone myself just to hear that great animal crash along, had it not been for my small daughter being ill," Big Pig replied.

I felt a new thrill at the thought of gaur or wild cattle living in these hills. Here was the ultimate big game as far as I was concerned, having wanted to hunt them since childhood. I was the small boy again, wanting to bag my first deer, and remembered how much it had meant to me to " graduate " from one kind of big game to the next. But I had a long trail to walk yet before reaching what is, in the Lahu hunters' code, a greenhorn hunter. Gaur had always evaded me the few times that I had been in country in which they were to be found.

When some of the hunters came over to the chief's fire, my first question was who the lucky hunter might be that could now be so distinguished. The name Ca Co Suh was mentioned as the man who got credit for slaying the big bull.

" But this is the hunter who doesn't need another bull *heh-nu* for credit," Big Pig explained. " With this bull he has killed ten times more than he needs to become a great hunter."

In a little while, I met the second Lahu who was to become another very good and close companion. Ca Co Suh, titled as " *Heh-nu baw pa* ", the Gaur Slayer, was a small, wiry man who did not place any importance to the business of washing. In the thousand or more days that we later spent together, I never saw him bathe once. Perhaps he was right in his particular case that bathing made him get sick, because he never seemed to suffer even a cold and the bites of insects did not seem to worry him. Strangely, he always appeared quite clean except after butchering some big animal when he would go through a period of " letting the blood dry and crumble off ". He was strictly a hunter, one of a few who lived entirely off the trade of meat, horns, hides and " medicines " to be found from different parts of wild animals. His vigorous and prolonged handshake had transferred a good mess of old gaur blood to my own hand which I found myself rubbing off with a good deal of amusement. I remarked about this laughingly and said that I was now getting near to the gaur at last.

" I promise you, Jaw Maw, that you will soon smear *heh-nu* blood on your gunstock," Ca Co Suh said with a smile that was so spontaneous as to be alarming. I was to learn that beneath his usually grim, apparently angry exterior, he had a great sense of humour that matched his rough, unkempt appearance. It is perhaps a blessing that he speaks only Lahu, and somehow has an aversion to say much in the presence of ladies.

A dozen or more men and boys now joined us by the fireside after a quick wash at the stream. Some of them had even taken the pains to run a comb through their hair and put on a fresh shirt. Ca Co Suh looked around at these with unconcealed disdain, while continuing his private little game of reaching around to various parts of his anatomy for troublesome ticks. He was producing astounding numbers of them, throwing each one carefully into the fire with the abandon of someone trimming and cleaning his fingernails.

" The ticks must be very bad this time of the year," I remarked.

" Not so bad as in a month or so," Ca Co Suh replied and with the same stolid, inscrutable expression added, " because by then the old nests of the wild boar dry up and the ticks start looking for me with more determination. Then I have to come back to camp, take off all my clothes and dance around through the flames like I was a fresh-plucked chicken needing to be singed!" He did not change his facial expression while all the men laughed at his joke, and continued thoughtfully staring into the flames of the campfire.

I could see that all the men liked this scarred and unwashed little man who knew how to joke, tell tall tales and shoot a gun or bow like the master that he was. I became very fond of him myself and as a little joke, gave him a nicely wrapped cake of soap each Christmas. These he used to swab out the bore of his muzzleloader, explaining that if he gave them to his wife or children, "they might develop the silly habit of washing with soap". Besides, wasn't it more important to keep the gun in good operational condition?

It had been an altogether grand reception for the grandson of the *Ah-pa-ku-lo,* who, much to my amusement, they now preferred to call *Jaw Maw.* This more or less has the equivalent of " Bwana " in the sense that my Lahu companions used it when speaking to me. We sat, throughout that night, munching wild beef and venison, and I listened to the many tales that these second- and even third-generation converts of my grandfather had to relate. The Japanese invasion during 1942-1945 had scattered even these mountain folk, and resulted in a number of social changes. For one thing, their original numbers moved off in groups to join other Lahu societies, so that few groups could now be found containing all Christians. This had the effect of modifying many members of the original villages with a touch of the animism that prevails in the majority of Lahu villages.

Now was a time to meet again, and the " Children of the Hills and Vales " had much to tell me, as I had to tell them. Surely, I thought, it had been less of a chance reunion than a destiny that *had* to be fulfilled. In any case, I knew that my own wanderings had brought me to beginnings of trails that I had never yet explored, and which were about to lead me to fulfilment of many dreams that I had entertained since childhood. I was about to pick up where my father and grandfather had left off, although I would not be walking with the missionary's spirit, but rather with the spirit of the adventurer and explorer that had also possessed my forebears to an intense degree.

When I found myself sitting once more by a campfire with friends whose very lives were based upon junglelore, I was completely happy again. Had I tried to sleep that night, I doubt that I could have done so. The excitement of the day before still gripped me when a rooster tried to crow from its cramped position in a basket. A dozen of the men had remained by the campfire all night, and the strong green tea we had been drinking went along with a solid round of conversation. I listened to Big Pig and several of the others describe their many guerilla experiences which had been organised by various Lahu leaders against the Japanese. These had been highly successful engagements which, collectively, contributed to the final defeat suffered by the Japanese.

" They tried to find us in our own jungles, and we had to kill them in unfair battle. They should never have tried that," Big Pig reflected at one point. " We might have left them alone, except that they became foolish at times and took revenge by murdering some of our innocent people. So we ambushed them again and again, taking their weapons and ammunition, and of seven hundred Lahu warriors I know, each had at least been ' blooded ' once."

In my turn, I told them about my stay in India where I had waited out the main duration of the war after parting from the Lahu. I was then too young to take part in the war, but had been able to take time out between school sessions to roam the Himalayas and to hunt. The Lahu men listened with interest as I told them about the strange

23

animals found in India: *nilghai, goral, hurrin, chinkara, bhurrahl,* and *tahr* for which the Lahu had no names. And they thought it very odd that the Hindu religion did not allow its adherents to eat the meat of animals, or that the Moslem man would pass up wild pork.

As a child, I had known little about the United States, having been there only once at the age of seven. Now I could answer more questions about the land of many automobiles and tall buildings. Such points, however, required only brief descriptions, mainly because they were quite beyond vivid understanding to the Lahu. There had to be much more said about the forests and wild animals in the North American woods. They thought it incredible that the United States had mountains and forests at all, having assumed that the country was all one great city. I tried to give them some sort of understanding about what America was really like, ending up with an explanation on how the world was really round instead of being flat. All this must be true, one of the men had suggested, because if a man went deep into a cave and listened long and carefully, the faint voices of people living on the other side of the world could be heard!

The ice and snow of such places as Korea and Alaska were difficult for them to understand, as were my attempts to describe the great expanses of water that separate continents. And so we had found it more profitable to talk about the forest and hunting strange game in strange places, and well-known game in unusual circumstances. It had been a hunters' campfire, and I found myself relishing every minute of that night. The dawning of the new day, unlike any that I had ever awaited, came on almost unnoticed. I could not have cared less; it seemed quite unnecessary.

The whole camp seemed to come to life the moment that the pale light of dawn penetrated the shaded areas where the many silent lean-tos had stood. Little naked boys dashed out to pass water against the handiest tree, then came running up the slope to see what the men were still talking about around the fire. Some of them were immediately recalled by mothers to fetch water in long bamboo joints from the stream below. Smoke from the numerous cooking fires soon swelled up to lie lazily under the canopy of tall trees. Four young hunters came by, shook hands with me, and told me that they would probably miss my departure. I wanted to join them on that exciting early morning round of the grazing spots, but instead, decided to make my way back to my little camp some three miles down the ridge.

A delicious breakfast followed, prepared by Big Pig's wife, consisting of fern sprouts fried together with finely chopped gaur meat. The rice was fragrant and large-grained, a mountain variety which is the choice of hill people. As I ate together with Big Pig and several of the men, I looked again more closely at my hosts.

Here were the real *Mussuh,* or "Hunters" as the Shans called them, coming from rather obscure ethnic origins of the complicated maze of Tibeto-Burman peoples. The *Lahu-na* tribe must be separated from a number of closely-related tribes, when speaking of their prowess as hunters and of their thorough knowledge of nature. While others have limitations to names of the things of the jungles, the Lahu has carried out a systematic description —a taxonomy—which gives names to nearly all things, both large and small. The *Akha* tribe, for instance, are keen enough hunters and trappers, but most of them recognise only three kinds of ants in the jungles: big, medium and small. The Lahu have intricate names for thirty or more species, grouped into five or six generic classifications. This is *Pu-waw-na-je-le,* they say, belonging to the family of *Na-je-le.* A Lahu, far from his native forest areas where unfamiliar forms of life and vegetation is found, is apt to spend a great deal of time trying to identify what appears to him as new species or subspecies of anything from barely visible insects to great trees. He readily understands the natural scientist's desire to discover new things. It is the rare Lahu whose memory is not good enough to recall what type of exotic blossoms a certain small orchid, looking very much the same as many others in the plant itself, will have when it comes to bloom once every three years. Some of the best orchid guides I ever had were small boys around twelve years old.

Most of these men would be considered small by western standards as well as their women who average less than five feet in height. They are sturdy, light-brown complexioned people whose most spectacular muscular development lies in the legs from constant mountain climbing. Many of the men show faces which suggest a distant kinship to the Mongols; the high cheek-bones, the fold over the eyes, and a wisp of a moustache at the sides of the upper lip. They might well have come from the hordes of the Great Khan, but the sharper features of the face are harder to place; some say that remnants of mercenaries from the armies of Alexander the Great somehow reached and mixed with the wild tribal women of southern China; or had it been that Kublai Khan brought back Caucasian women from the west? Whatever the actual origins with its many mixings of blood, these people came from many generations of highland hunters who found the deep forests to their liking.

I watched Big Pig as he sat or squatted by the fireside, his knee-length, loose cotton pants drawn back to expose hard, sinewy thigh muscles over which ran a long and ragged scar from the tusk of a wild boar. Numerous other scars told the story of bullets and knives, claws and fangs, and the smallpox which had nearly killed him in youth.

The sun was rising steadily higher in the east; it was time that I took leave of these people and try to complete the long drive home in the afternoon.

"Over there," Big Pig said, pointing to the south-east, "that's where we will go in two weeks."

I followed the direction of his gaze to the massive blue-grey mountain formations, far across the Fang valley. These had fascinated me as I came up from Chiengmai two days before, so I had stopped to ask villagers at Mae Khi about them. "Doi Vieng Pha," The Mountain City of Cliffs, they had explained, where hunters did not go because of many evil spirits which are believed to haunt the summits. And what about the big game up there? "Ho! Many, many big animals, *kating*, tiger, bear, sambar and wild elephant," a wizened old farmer cackled. All I needed after that were men willing to go with me. I was thrilled that Big Pig planned to go there anyway, spirits or no spirits. When I told him about what the valley folks had said he laughed.

"If Lisu hunters can go there, so can we. The kind of spirits mountain people worry about are not the same as those that bother the valley people," he chuckled. "In fact, those same spirits usually *like* mountain people! But the Lisu who have been there said that there is a strange jinx on Doi Vieng Pha which I think we should go and discover for ourselves."

In two weeks, I knew, Big Pig and his people would have completed moving into their new village site and there would then be time to join them for a long trip. I made plans to join them at a point on the main Fang-Chiengmai road from which it seemed that a suitable course could be followed into the Doi Vieng complex. It would be a first trip for all of us, and I detected the keen anticipation in Big Pig's words which made me thrill the more that I had found the right companions. The thrill of discovery motivated these people as much as it did me. I wondered if I would be able to contain my eagerness long enough to get through the next two weeks. As I was to find out in our later associations together, Big Pig was

27

good at summing up my own feelings as well as his at different times.

"Ah, Jaw Maw," he had intoned just as we took leave of each other on that first meeting, " our trails have met on this little ridge. It is very good. No mountains can be too high, or valleys too deep when we can share the walk together into new places."

CHAPTER TWO

The Jinxed Mountain

" Te tzuh te maw la meh
Te Hk'aw te maw la meh."

A Speck at first glance,
May be a mountain instead.

E ARLY on the morning of the third day, I was given
a reward over and above my highest expectations. A
short way from the camp that we had made the
evening before on the west slope of Doi Vieng Pha, the
sharp ridge of the summit separated two worlds. Big Pig
and I stood quite speechless as we gazed at the panorama
over the whole eastern side of Doi Vieng Pha. We had
come there at precisely the right moment as the sun's
golden glow spread over the land.

What a land! Numerous grass-topped and gently sloping
ridges dropped away to a rushing river some two miles off
to our right, to rise again on the opposite bank into another
and another series of ridges. Verdant forests of hardwoods
and bamboo covered the ridgesides and valleys. The mur-
mur of many streams could be heard over the din of dozens
of family groups of whooping gibbon apes. I had dreamed
of it, but had never been in such a hunters' paradise. The
gruelling ten-hours of solid climbing the day before seemed
a very small price to pay even for five minutes' eye-feasting
of such a land.

I pointed to the dark specks, a thousand yards away,
and as I turned excitedly to Big Pig, he nodded. " Yes,

heh-nu," he said, " and there, more *heh-nu,* a big bull, five, six, seven cows, and *Khui-zuh* (Sambar) on that ridge! This is a place for hunters! "

Even at this great distance, pearly horns gleamed and flashed occasionally as the great animals grazed undisturbed in the morning sun, dark bodies standing out against the white of dew-covered grass. I felt a bubbling joy and thrill that made me want to sing and jump, but tried to appear calm, even as Big Pig, the great Lahu hunter, not given to showing his emotions while inwardly he experienced the same such thrills.

Leaning my rifle against a gnarled little shrub, I sat down on a damp rock. My Lahu companion fumbled in his bag for his pipe, still gazing intently at the herd of gaur. The pleasure of stalking and tracking a big bull could wait; the whole day lay ahead for hunting. I filled the bowl of my own pipe, lit it, and watched as more and more of the grand panorama emerged from purple shadows of the dawn to verdant hues as far as the eye could see. " The Mountain City of Cliffs " was, in fact, nothing more than the long escarpment of cliffs which walled in this beautiful land beyond. Viewed from the Fang plain, all that one saw was this great wall which rose to six thousand feet from a valley of around a thousand feet in elevation. Its location, almost on the centre of northern Thailand, commands a 360-degree view, on clear days, of the entire northern part of the kingdom. The borders of Laos, far to the east, and Burma to the north and west can be seen beyond the fertile, rice-growing valleys of Thailand's northern provinces.

The valley folk say that a host of demons and evil spirits live in this " city " to claim the lives of unwise hunters who venture there. Around the top, Doi Vieng is indeed a forbidding place during the long rainy season, shrouded by gloomy clouds and damp from mists nine months of the year. Its dark forests of twisted, wind-tortured trees,

and the wailing winds which cross the jagged rocks, lend
a likely setting in which the timid soul can imagine an
assortment of ghosts. At night, in the eerie half-light of
the moon, the sounds are unreal, distorted, yet amplified
by the winds which give weird animation to the grotesque,
bending trees. Instead of spirits, the ghostly forms of tiger
nightly prowl the ridgelines, voicing their deep roars
where other animals avoid the ridge-trail.

Below this windswept crest are primeval glades beneath
great moss-laden trees. Here, the deep layers of decaying
litter generates a clammy warmth, and at rare times, rays
of sunlight beam down through the thick foliage, attempt-
ing, yet never fulfilling their mission to dry. In these
moments, there is a sudden revival of insect activity as
myriad small wings flash in and out of the sun's rays,
absorbing briefly the sun's short-lived victory. Palm-like
Cycads, which once dominated the earth's vegetation,
stand here and there beneath giant trees. In the glades
there is no breeze to move even the supple tree ferns, or
the Phyllodendra and Lycopodia which cover the tree
trunks as far as the first branches.

The spectacle above arrests the attention longest. Like
a moss, whole limbs are covered by millions of fine-
blossomed miniature orchids, scenting the glade with their
fragrance. Here and there, splashes of brilliant colours
mark the larger orchids. The famous *Vanda coerulea,* with
four-inch blossoms of exotic deep blue, are as prevalent
as more common Dendrobia and Cymbidia. There are
golds and yellows, purples and reds, and variegated com-
binations of whites nestled among the mossy burdens of
each branch.

The greater balance of Doi Vieng's terrain consists of
well-drained ridges which are carpeted with grass and
bracken. A kind of wild vetch-like legume entwines the

soft grasses, affording rich natural pastures to gaur,*
sambar deer, wild pig, elephant and serao.† The valleys
are forest-covered, becoming dense with rattan and bamboo along the streams. Whole sections are often covered
with wild bananas, typically trampled by elephants which
forage there for the tender inner stalks.

Leaving our delightful look-out point, Big Pig and I
crossed the first valley near its head, well above the wild
cattle which now moved slowly towards the cover of
bamboo below. The large bull with the seven cows continued grazing on the slope two ridges beyond this first
herd that we had seen. There seemed to be a good chance
that we might reach the second herd before it followed the
advice of the rising sun to take off into dense cover. I
followed Big Pig, who was setting a wild pace down through
brackens that whipped and tripped me.

A half-hour later, we poked cautiously over the last
ridge beyond which the herd had been seen grazing. I
was primed to shoot my first bull gaur, trying to calm
myself for a steady shot. We drew a complete blank. Where
massive bodies had stood on the slope no more than fifteen
minutes before, a lone barking deer doe moved out across
the open, sniffing suspiciously at the gaur scent left on
the grass. She spotted us immediately and stood frozen in
the middle of the clearing, trying to determine what kind
of strange animals we might be without the benefit of our
scent coming to her. Heavy with fawn, she trotted awkwardly down the slope and as soon as she had gained the
bamboos, gave three sharp barks. When in doubt, run
for cover. Big Pig grinned his amusement and started out
over the ridge to study the tracks of the gaur.

" The bull in this herd is big, but not as big as this
one that passed through here two days ago," he said,

* *Bibos gaurus*, referred to as *Kating* (Thai) or " Gaur " in these
accounts, largest living species of bovine.
† *Capricornis*, a large goat-antelope.

ABOVE: A fine specimen of a Bull Gaur
(*Bos gaurus*)

BELOW (*left*): A buck Barking Deer
(Muntjac) with matured horns.

BELOW (*right*): A doe Barking Deer,
curious yet distrustful.

A fine Sambar Stag of about four years.

A young Sambar buck and a doe.

ABOVE, *left*: A baby Stumptail, which can be the cause of much trouble to the troup in the jungles. ABOVE, *right*: A matured Pig-tailed Macaque looking docile enough.

A tusker in open forest eyes the intruder.

The live buck Barking Deer needs careful handling, since it is capable of terrible fang slashing. Little Pig holds a buck that has been tranquillised for shipping to the Chiengmai Zoo.

ABOVE: A male otter peers with interest at the camera.

LEFT: A young boar, tusks just developing.

ABOVE: A Reticulated Python, which was just large enough to require both hands to hold it.

RIGHT: A specimen of the Warrior Wasp or Hornet, actual size.

A male Great Hornbill approaches its nest.

ABOVE: A Green Fruit pigeon, one of the great music makers.

LEFT: The "Coppersmith" Barbet, tireless little songster.

A flight of Wreathed Hornbills going across
leaden monsoon skies in the early morning.

ABOVE, *left*: A Yao tribesman with his home-made muzzle-loading shotgun, powder horn and shot bag. ABOVE, *right*: Meo elder and his waterpipe.

Li Co, one of the few Lahu-na hunters
who has earned his supreme hunting
reputation with the bow alone.

Big Pig, the intrepid mountain man and
his famous muzzle-loading rifle.

A Red Lahu girl from the more southerly
complex of Red Lahu groups.

P'wo Karen girls dressed for courting.

BELOW, *left*: A Black Lahu, or Lahu-na girl in traditional costume. BELOW, *right*: A Red Lahu maiden of the northern Red Lahu group.

A Lahu village high on the Mak-Ang-Khang range.

Red Lahu villagers at a small hamlet near the Burma border.

Whey Mi Lahu hunters, carrying Gaur horns and meat to sell, met while the author was going to their village.

ABOVE: The big killer bear of Whey Mi which had killed and mauled a number of Lahu in the area.

BELOW, *left*: The author with New Soul, Little Pig and Solid Log. They are laughing over New Soul's gibbon fur hat, which he also uses as a game bag.

BELOW, *right*: New Soul cocking a very powerful Lahu hunting crossbow.

Na-lao Lisu man with "author's tiger", one which had eluded the author for over a year.

"Lena" and the author's daughter, Julie, shortly before the young leopard became too much to handle.

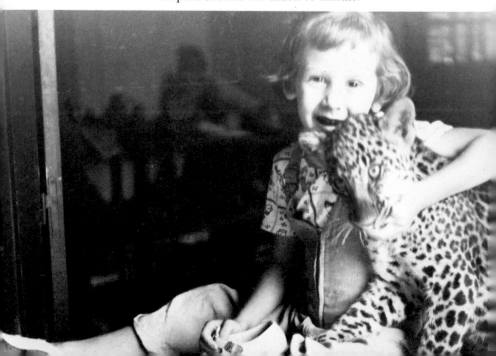

pointing out a hoofprint as wide as my two hands together. Ground spiders had woven webs across the sharp depressions left by the bull's hoofs, and the weeds lay withered where they had been pressed into the damp soil. All around these old prints were the fresh tracks of the herd we had seen and the steam still rose from a great pile of fresh dung.

"If this was the last day here, I would be glad to take a young cow from this herd so that we can take home the sweet, tender meat. But we are just started, and the great horns of the big lone bull beckon me strongest," Big Pig said, trying to decide what we should do. I agreed that we should take our time and try for the best bull possible. "Sure, shop around first," I thought, "and don't buy the first and easiest thing." Doi Vieng had many herds of gaur; it shouldn't be hard to find a beautiful bull in the trophy class.

Big Pig led the way, following the old tracks down towards the stream. We were off to a good start and I was feeling in such good spirits that I eschewed my usual oaths each time a mass of sticky cobwebs wrapped around my face, temporarily pinning my eyelashes together. The headwaters of the Mae Fang rushed with a steady roar below, dynamic, refreshing and pulsing the air with vitality. There was promised adventure in the air, I was happy to be alive and fit and in this place, and innocently unaware of the "jinx" of Doi Vieng. Had I known of this "jinx" that we all came to believe in later, I would have left the Doi Vieng herds of gaur alone. While I shall never regret the many days spent on Doi Vieng, "*a-tryin' to catch the devil's herd,*" and the many gallons of sweat I left there, I will never be satisfied as to why I could not find my bull gaur in the most likely of all places. I came upon gaur in the most unlikely of situations later. There could be only one explanation; Doi Vieng *is* jinxed.

The stream had been hidden from view by tall *mai sang* bamboos. As we stepped out into the clearing under this canopy and saw the stream for the first time, I wanted immediately to see our camp moved to that spot. It was an ideal location, far superior to the hastily selected spot of the evening before just as it had been getting dark. I was about to say this to Big Pig when a " boulder " in the streambed moved. The big boar stood, up to its belly in the water, still unaware of our presence thirty yards behind him as he rooted at the far bank. Glancing quickly at Big Pig, I saw that he was saying, " Shoot, shoot " with his mouth. I raised my rifle slowly, took steady aim at a spot just behind the ear, and I doubt that old boar ever knew what stopped his rooting so suddenly. Big Pig Oh-ho-hoed happily and we strode quickly over to where the boar lay in the water. He had magnificent tusks and enough meat to keep three times the number of men in our party gorged for days. And camp would be made right here. I started butchering while Big Pig went for the other Lahu men.

I took off my boots and waded out to the half-submerged boar. His four-hundred-odd pounds were too much to drag, so I commenced to dissect and move him, a limb at a time, to banana leaves which I had placed on the bank. My job completed, I stripped and enjoyed an icy bath in the headwaters of the Mae Fang, 5,000 feet above and seventy miles from the nearest village along its long course to the Mae Khong (Mekhong) river.

In about two hours, the six Lahu men came silently through the bamboos. They carried individual rattan baskets with accustomed ease, springing along lightly on sturdy and muscular legs, and with pants rolled tightly up to the hips. Big Pig had retrieved his ungainly muzzle-loader, carrying it cradled across his right arm. They filed over to a choice spot and set their basket packs down, then came over to make cheery comments about our windfall of meat. Each in turn admired the boar's tusks then turned to start in on making the camp where we would remain for the next six days.

Besides Big Pig, their young and able chief, the other five were: Ca Co Suh, " New Soul "; Teh K'u, " Solid Log "; Sheh Hpu, " Luck-to-find-gems "; Ca Va Eh, " Little Pig "; and Ca Nu Pa, " Stud Bull ". These six were among the most intrepid men of the jungles that I have ever met, each with his own incredible experiences and lovable personality. New Soul I have mentioned already as the " Gaur Slayer " who does not think that bathing is important. Solid Log, the only member who could read and write a little from mission school days, was a bow-maker unparalleled. Gems, for short, could call in a controlled falsetto just like a gibbon, and he had large, prominent eyes which were as sharp as those of a hawk. Little Pig was in fact a small man with skills in tracking that cannot be equalled. Stud Bull, fluent speaker of seven languages and dialects, had a fantastic record of having been the most-travelled Lahu I ever met. At different times he had been a guerilla fighter, opium smuggler, police scout, bus boy (which he hated) and great lover of many lovely ladies. He started off being the cook and at this he was superb. Of all the hillpeople that I have met from that day to this, Stud Bull will remain longest in my memories because he has been my beloved friend and faithful personal servant to this day.

On this first visit to Doi Vieng Pha, I came to understand something of the Lahu's inner nature. Their love for the *yeh*, or high rain forest, is even deeper-rooted than the original animism itself. It is from such settings that their songs and ballads have come, nourished into beautiful poetry by constant exposure to and observation of the things of Nature around them. While professing a kind of simple Christianity, many of Big Pig's people followed animistic practices peculiar to the Lahu. Their's is a sort of theistic animism which includes one God, Creator of all things and Keeper of all ordered life. All earthly woes are a result of the many foul spirits which seek to undermine the good things of life and man's attempts to do anything at all. The Great God, *G'uisha*, is unapproachable, but it is said that if man might meet *G'uisha* at all, he would have to appear somewhere in the *yeh* where man has not yet desecrated the beauty of original creation. Consonant with the beauty and purity of the *yeh*, the Lahu's *G'uisha* was conceived to be pure and good, kind and loving, and such concepts could not have been influenced by Christian suggestion. Every Lahu, consciously or otherwise, looks for his *G'uisha* in the *yeh*; for the *yeh* is in fact his heaven.

In a short time our new camp had been established, complete with banana-leaf lean-tos. A pot of rice boiled over three stones and Stud Bull peeled the outer sheaths away from a section of banana stalk for the white, inner meat as vegetable to go along with the boar meat. Big Pig and I sat munching roasted boar liver, and discussed plans for locating the big bull gaur.

For a sporting arm, I had but one rifle then, a ·30/06 Springfield. It has always remained my favourite rifle, although it needs desperately to be retired. Big Pig carried the only other gun, a muzzle-loading ancient which has the faint inscription " Tower 1865 ", possibly having reached this part of the world, almost a century ago, by the hand of pirates or traders. Of this scarred and worn old weapon, Big Pig said, " So close a friend as this, a man cannot trade for five pony-loads of silver or ten young maidens! " It was a famous piece even before it reached my friend's hands. Since the time his father had passed it on to him, Big Pig had established records for big game that few could match. His favourite tale concerned a tiger which was stopped instantly at over a hundred yards with a ball through the eye. In any case it had been a fine shot, aimed at the tiger's head. His modest conclusion, always followed by a hearty laugh: "A great shot it was, but it disappoints me to recall that I aimed for the right eye and hit him in the left!"

Right after our early lunch, Big Pig and Little Pig started out to take the right side of our planned " V " prod and I took the left direction accompanied by New Soul. We were well inside the usual foraging area of the several different herds of wild elephant that roamed the region. Game trails criss-crossed the dense slopes right up to the top of the far ridgeline, and on the steeper climbs elephant had established " slides " which gave them a shortcut on the descent to the stream below. During the rains the huge beasts, almost playfully, would sit on their ample behinds with front legs extended and slide for a hundred yards or more, making wide tracks and frightening away all other animals in the vicinity. New Soul and I climbed laboriously up the last slide near the top and found where the bull gaur had crossed the day before. He had come from our right, the direction in which Big Pig had gone. We followed the tracks for about a quarter of a mile and felt reasonably sure that the flat ridge some three miles to the east was his destination. We abandoned the tracks there and started back to camp.

An hour after we reached camp, the two men returned from the right fork. Little Pig described with excited gestures their meeting with wild elephant just a mile from camp. " See that limb there? The big bull was *that* high! " he claimed with emphatic gusto.

Gems gaped in mock wonderment. "Ah, I believe he was probably *that* tall," he replied, pointing to a lower limb. " Little Pig, from your position so close to the ground, the bull looked taller, that is what happened! "

The little man took it good-naturedly. " Have it your way, you long-legged stork! But when the Little Pig says it was big, you had better believe it was big! "

" I was badly tempted to shoot him, Jaw Maw," Big Pig

mused as he turned to me. " If he had a few more kilos of tusk than he did, I could have done business with the ivory carver in Fang."

" It is best that we leave the ivory alone and stay friends with Thai law," I replied, recalling the rigid penalties this country has for killing wild elephant. It is necessary for a man, even in self-defence, to establish definite proof for killing an elephant before the courts can exonerate him. It is, however, more truly a moral law, the wild elephant being accepted as national symbols and property of His Majesty the King. The remote tribesman is usually unable to see it in that light. To him the ivory is still worth a great deal when shadily passed to an illegal dealer. Fortunately, all tribesmen still do not realise that, and relatively few elephant are killed each year in Thailand. With steadily improving game laws and enforcement, it is foreseeable that the great herds within this Kingdom will be preserved as they deserve to be.

Dinner that evening was superb and I congratulated Stud Bull and his helper, Gems. The wild pork had been prepared in three different fashions, with two of the dishes fried in their own fat. Vegetables consisted of palm heart, banana flower, water ferns, and banyan sprouts. We ate like kings, topping the meal off with delicious wild figs. The only items we had brought from home had been rice, salt and onions. Wild ginger, pulled up ten yards from the campfire, had been used for seasoning. Even wild tea was available for the picking, and this the men brewed straight from the green leaves.

After dinner, we sat around a second campfire which we called a " pleasure " fire, adding several more chapters to the thousands of tales we exchanged around such fires. I looked up at the clear December sky through a gap in the tall bamboos overhead. Stars winked brilliantly from Orion's belt and I felt that " The Hunter " was smiling on us with good omen. We paused in our happy yarn-spinning only to listen to the sounds of the night around us. A mile to the west, but sounding much closer, a tigress " boomed " two-syllable roars at frequent intervals, impatiently in heat too early in the season. She was answered by an even more majestic "Aaah—Ooom!" from Doi Vieng's main ridge. When the two met, it would sound like a terrible battle, while the " affectionate " female scratched and screamed at her dutiful mate. There were periodic trumpetings from wild elephant, the startled dog-like cries of a barking deer (*Muntjac*) and the hoots, screeches and clear, flute-like calls of the different owls.

As thoughts turned to the night's sleep, an indescribable bellowing came echoing down the ravine from our left. It was difficult to identify at once and we listened carefully as the long, drawn-out sound came a second and a third time.

" It is a bear," Little Pig said.

Gems differed. "A sound like that can come only from some terrible demon," he announced, eyes wide and very serious.

Calmly Big Pig raised his hand to gain our attention and the voice of experience gave the explanation. " Once before, when I was hunting the Nam Hsim river country, I heard such a call. It is the agony cry of a bull elephant which has either broken a tusk in battle or suffers bad wounds. Be wise, my brothers, and do not go near that one unless you want to be buried in many different graves!" My last thought as I snuggled into my sleeping bag was that I would avoid all wild elephant in the morning and as long as we remained on Doi Vieng.

On this mountain, the dewfall is made specially for the hunter, as New Soul said. Just at that critical time before dawn when preparations should be made for a day's hunt, the dew saturates the bamboo leaves above and begins to drop like a gentle rain. Solid Log unceremoniously snatched the wide banyan leaf under which Little Pig was completely hidden, curled up like a happy squirrel. " Up, Beautiful Sleeper! The rains have begun and you sleep like a field mouse! "

" Ha! Away from your master. Go find wastes to eat at the edge of the village! " Little Pig sat up, addressing a meddlesome dog. In the next instant he had leaped up, grabbed Solid Log playfully and tossed the much bigger man easily to the ground. " Next time you destroy a good dream, I will toss you clear up into the branches of that banyan tree! " he said, pretending terrible anger, then ran laughing towards the stream.

Big Pig pulled out his long knife to cut away an occasional trailer of rattan as Little Pig and I followed. The game trail which we used was barely visible when we left the camp and remained dark for a time as we passed through the valley. When we left the shelter of bamboos and started through the tall grass, we were soaked in a few minutes from the waist down by the dew. An hour later we had traversed the top of the valley which New Soul and I had reached the day before, continuing rapidly along towards the flat ridge beyond. Had we been interested in lesser game than gaur, a beautiful sambar stag, which sprang up out of the broomgrass near the ridgetop, might have made a fine trophy. The sun was well up over the ragged escarpments to the east by the time we began the steep climb to the flat ridge we had marked as a likely spot for the bull's bedding grounds. His two-and-three-day-old tracks were plentiful along old trails which elephant had established. Still, there were no fresh tracks.

It was necessary to circle the ridge from about three hundred yards below the flat place, so that we would be able to approach upwind. Thus we came into the flat area, some five acres in size, from the opposite direction to our original course from camp, with the sun behind us. Here the gaur's tracks informed us that he had a definite preference for this area, since his fresh tracks, together with that of a great bull elephant, led towards the flatland. I saw Big Pig frown, then look back towards our camp, taking a bearing of our position.

" Pierce my nose, and put a steel ring through it if I am wrong. These are the tracks of that bull elephant we heard last night, the one with the long cry!" he said.

"The bull gaur steps in his tracks, so we should not find the elephant here," Little Pig reasoned, eager that we should not abandon this promising tracking for an elephant that we did not care to meet.

Remember what they say about Doi Vieng," he said, " it is a mountain upon which the spirits have cast spells! " He paused, listening carefully. "We must move noiselessly now." Big Pig was being persuaded against his better judgement to proceed directly into the low bamboos which covered the flat ahead.

I looked at the elephant tracks, huge, dwarfing the gaur tracks which by themselves were most impressive. I felt that my companions might be unduly concerned about meeting the ill-disposed elephant because the tracks appeared to me as more than twenty-four hours old. Besides, I reasoned with myself, we should hear a great, noisy beast like this if he remained anywhere near us. The gaur's tracks were very fresh, perhaps no more than a few hours, and the possibility of meeting it soon dispelled any apprehensions I had about the elephant. Following Little Pig's quiet tracking, I was certain that each moment was bringing us closer to an unforgettable meeting with the gaur of all gaurs, which must be lying down just ahead, chewing leisurely on his cud. I thrilled to the thought of imminent encounter.

We had been moving along under *mai lai* bamboos for about fifteen minutes, stooping very low and practically on all fours. The area had been well-trampled by wild elephant and gaur, leaving broken and twisted bamboo stalks to obstruct the trail. The big game simply walked over these; we had to crawl under most of them in order to avoid noise. It was as bad a place as any to meet a charging animal. Visibility averaged about twenty feet, escape routes were practically nil, and a man could get badly lacerated on the sharp edges of cracked bamboo. I had been mulling all of these factors with considerable ease when I saw Little Pig's hand go up in a signal to " freeze."

Without a word, he indicated by pointing his thumb ahead and slightly to our right, then touched his ear to tell me that he had heard something. The three of us crouched a yard apart, one behind the other, straining our ears for a full minute to hear some new sound. Then a dull " clunk, clunk " came unmistakably from the direction that Little Pig had indicated. I nodded recognition to Little Pig and inched past him for a better view through the close bamboos. It seemed to me that the sound could be no other than that of a bull gaur rubbing his horn against a tree, and each time the clunking started again, I moved forward a few more paces. What rare good luck! We had the bull by surprise or he would not be indulging in this bit of relaxed horn shining. Now, I had only to slip forward until I saw him, make no noise and take my time. It would be as easy as that to score at last on the elusive gaur. I found myself even concerned over the fact that I might not obtain a good photograph of the big bull, once I had him, because of the thick bamboos. I was counting a lot of chickens that would never hatch.

The clunking sounds stopped abruptly and an unfamiliar squeal, high-pitched and pig-like made me stop in bafflement. I wanted to see what the reactions of my companions were, but I could not see them from my position some five yards ahead. The squealing kept up for about ten seconds then changed to a rumbling, like the sound of distant rolling thunder. So these were the strange things about gaur that I had yet to learn. Or was I so excited that my ears were deceiving me? I knew that I was in a state of high tension and my nerves were doing their best to render my senses unreliable.

Peering under the bamboos, I had an opening that extended about ten yards along the game trail. Two dark pillars rose from the ground, too close together to be tree trunks, and disappeared into the thick leaves above. Just above the first layer of leaves I saw a glint of white, then a movement that was part of a great, flapping ear. Bit by bit, a " mountain " materialised, and I gaped in awe at the biggest living creature that I have seen in the jungles—enormous because it was so close to me! My " gaur " turned out to be the bull elephant.

Suddenly the trunk shot up, immediately followed by a blasting trumpet, so loud and shrill that I reeled backwards, numbed with consternation and shock. My companions were yelling loudly, almost hysterically, but their warnings were meaningless mouthings. The bamboos were already flying apart and the elephant loomed huge as he came crashing through directly at me.

Later, I could look back at it and laugh at my feeble initial reactions to make a bid for life in the face of devastating attack. I learned that, under those particular circumstances, I for one did not know where the trigger of my rifle was or even how the weapon functioned. In fact, I could not seem to find my rifle! I also learned that, just before I am to be crushed to death, I do not stand up and puff out my chest to await it. I cringe, I am terribly frightened and the best I can do is to raise my hand before my face. If you are too frightened, then a scream is incapable of coming forth. In those three or four seconds I knew human frailty, but I also came to understand something new about myself: I was capable of a quick change in reactions. This was extremely important to me and gave me new confidence which would remain.

The bull was three yards from me when I executed a

long horizontal dive to the right of the direction of charge. I must say that this was a beautiful dive, with my rifle extended straight out in front of me in my right hand. I give the credit to my old gym instructor back in college, and consider that the number of barrels I might have cleared should have won me a place on the team. It surely saved my life.

As the bull thrashed by in a heaving of bamboos just behind me, I heard a loud whack. He had swung his trunk at my flying form only to have it deflected off the stalks of bamboos. I landed half on the ground and half suspended upon the piled-up debris of fallen bamboo. From this position I quickly slithered and scrambled to a small open spot on the other side. When I stood up again, I realised at once that the bull had checked his charge some ten yards away and had already turned into a second charge, bellowing fearfully. This time I did not wait for him. As soon as I realised that he was making a straight course for me, I took a few steps away from his direction of charge, and ducked sharply around to the right behind a thick clump of bamboo. This time I had a good look at the old boy as he moved by like a locomotive. I stopped myself, just in time, from putting a poorly placed bullet somewhere in that huge anatomy. It was more of a gesture of nervous defiance on my part and might have only made matters worse. I was badly rattled, to say the least, and having a desperate time trying to figure my way out of the predicament.

This time, the bull stopped at the end of his charge, having turned and faced in my general direction. He had apparently not seen me behind the bamboos, and might have concluded that I had disappeared. But the concern of my two companions for my safety, despite its good intentions, nearly cost me my life again within the few minutes since the first charge. I was then standing quietly behind the clump of bamboos at a point directly between the bull and the two Lahus. They were, of course, not at all certain that I had survived the two passes from the bull and were yelling various suggestions to me, including what I should do if I was already dead! Little Pig's voice was full of woe: "If you can't move, then just lie very still!" That was *most* helpful, and I would have smiled under other circumstances. Big Pig, a little to the right of the other Lahu, was somewhat irrational himself for the only time since I have known him: "Shoot him, Jaw Maw, shoot him! Don't forget to shoot him!"

In exasperation, I shouted back a most annoyed "Shut up!" and immediately invited a third thrashing, crashing charge. I tried to make for my original position, which was less dense than the area to my right, in an attempt to get out of the bull's way. I ran into a maze of criss-crossing bamboo stalks and had to turn briefly into the direction from which the bull was coming before I could cut away again to the left. The bull definitely saw me just then and curved his charge slightly to include me as I fled to his right. Again, the same whack of the heavy trunk just behind my back, but fortunately striking bamboos, several dead pieces of which broke into sections, hitting me on the shoulder. And again I described another tumbling dive to gain that crucial yardage from the smashing feet. I made it! I found myself smiling foolishly and thinking momentarily that the game was finished. It even seemed that there was no further need to scramble away again until I had caught my breath. For a few seconds, I sat where my dive had landed me, rubbing a rip on my right forearm.

A tremendous blast suddenly informed me that the bull was not through. He continued his trumpeting until it was a repeat of the long call we had heard the previous evening. It was an indescribably terrible cry which must have included everything in elephant language that properly describes a bull's anger, frustration and hatred for human intruders. He was standing over the spot from which the three of us had separated, systematically trampling the place which still had our scent. I took this opportunity to strike out as quietly as possible for the more open space ahead of me. As I did so, Big Pig used very good judgement this time to assist me by whooping and whistling from a tall tree up which he had scrambled like a monkey, and getting down from which he had an extremely hard time later on! He had seen from his high perch that the bull was now between himself and me, and managed by his various noises to distract the bull long enough to allow me time to reach the open.

A large fallen log loomed up before me just where the tall grass dominated the bamboos. I jumped upon it and cat-walked along it until I had a clear view towards the elephant. The bull stood, just twenty yards away, looking squarely at me with head raised above the low bamboos. He was enormous and, for the first time, I could see the massive tusks clearly. Had he not seen me climb onto the log, he would have investigated the noises still coming from Big Pig. These noises were now saying, " *Baw lo, Jaw Maw, Baw lo*! (shoot now!"). From the top, absolutely the top of another tree came a whistle—Little Pig—making like a squirrel trying to get out of shotgun range. The trunk was large and smooth, presenting even monkeys with a real problem, and how the little man got up that tree will always remain a marvel to me. From this position, Little Pig had a squirrel's eye view of the whole event as it transpired right after his last whistles.

I had in my hands a ·30/06 rifle loaded with 220 grain soft-point bullets. Hunters the world over will agree, I'm sure, that I would have been better off with non-expanding ammunition, even Army " straight ball." The ·30/06 was certainly not my choice of rifle for the bull elephant which was then standing before me, ready to charge. I was holding my only rifle, my favourite for other reasons.

The bull came with trunk wrapped around his left

shoulder, ears back and moving smoothly like a great
whale cruising through the waves. I found myself suddenly
very calm as I raised my Springfield to take careful, almost
casual aim at a point just above the base of the trunk and
in line with the orifices of the ears. There I knew the
brain lay, deep behind the nasal cavity, and if my bullet
expanded too soon, on the bone, I might need to leap and
tumble all over again. But there would be a big difference
this time; the tall grass, over my head, was more perfect
for the elephant which could easily keep me located where-
ever I tried to move. He could course through the grass
as though it did not exist; I would find a thousand snares.
But my bullet penetrated the bone just anterior to the
brain, keeping its course instead of deflecting. My big bull
stopped in his tracks as though hit by a " solid " from an
approved elephant rifle. With a shudder, his knees buckled
and very much to my surprise, he crashed over on his left
side. I had expected to shoot several times, hoping at best
to turn the bull or cause him to sit down in the usual
fashion of elephant which have been hit, fatally or otherwise, in the head. But my great bull was down; his quivering legs told me that he was already dead. I was elated and
very proud of my beat-up old rifle. I had never wanted to
shoot an elephant and there was no satisfaction in this,
but there had been no definite assurance that I could
safely escape him otherwise.

A hearty " *Ah-lo-lo!* " came from Big Pig as he struggled
down his rough-barked oak, leaving some of his skin
behind and ripping the seams in the crotch of his pants. I
was standing by the dead elephant when my two companions joined me. Together we looked with wonder at
the small hole at the base of the trunk. Only a trickle of
blood oozed from the puncture and drained slowly down
to his left eye. The tusks seemed short, protruding only
some three feet, but they were massive. Later, the pair
scaled-out at sixty-four kilograms (about 140 lbs.), well up

to the maximums seen in Asiatic elephant. I have seen longer tusks from an Asiatic elephant which did not weigh as much.

It took the three of us about fifteen minutes to discover the reason for the bull's bad temper. For some reason, he had sustained a ghastly infection of the anus which was a mass of squirming maggots, pus and blood. His pain each time he passed excrement can be imagined. Possibly, the injury would never have healed and a slow, terrible death was in store for this magnificent creature. I felt that my bullet had performed a mission of mercy for the old bull, and had I known the true nature of his agonies, I would have sought him out with purpose, saving him the further exertion of those four memorable charges.

Like me, Big Pig was overwhelmed with the strange outcome of our gaur tracking. In all that great forest, the one animal we had vowed not to meet presented himself to us in this unforgettable way. Big Pig's words rang in my ears, " Remember that the spirits have cast spells . . ." I could appreciate the " Jinx " of Doi Vieng more fully after making nine subsequent visits. On none of these occasions was I able to take a bull gaur, the usual objective of my hunting. The " jinxed " nature of this mountain became so believable to my Lahu companions and me that it was in itself the challenge that brought us back again each time. To the best of my knowledge, the bulls on the " jinxed mountain " are still there, carrying trophy-class horns, somehow protected by the great dark mountain which overlooks the land.

CHAPTER THREE

The Stranger and the Bull of the Mae-Salak

" Hk'aw ta k'o mvuh hteh . . . Law ya k'o caw g'aw."
" On the hill lightning strikes . . . In the stream dragons attack."

THE old hunter had never been to the city, and just as he would have walked into any hillman's dwelling, he came unhesitatingly into the living room of my home and made himself comfortable by the fireside. Though I had never met him before, I was pleased that he had called on me and felt at ease to take a place at the hearth in the fashion of wayfaring tribesmen. It was a cold January night, one of the few times during the year when we would have a fire blazing merrily in the evening, and this lent just the right atmosphere for my visitor to feel more at home. I was glad he demonstrated a frank disregard for the dull and often meaningless social observances that more frequent visitors from the hills showed.

He felt no immediate need to introduce himself, nor to say anything at all for several moments. Because he felt more comfortable squatting by the fireplace, he sat thus instead of taking a chair that I offered. His dress was unconventional, yet it bore vaguely the cut and style of the Lisu tribe, and something about his serious, dignified bearing told me that he was a chieftain. According to tribal customs, the visitor is expected to speak first. I waited until he felt like speaking.

"I have come five days from Sam-muen mountain to see the horns which killed my brother," he announced finally, still gazing into the fire. "Do you have those horns?"

I had expected his Lahu to be heavily accented, but he spoke the dialect perfectly. There was only one bull gaur that he could have been referring to: a great bull from the Mae-Salak, just south of Sam-muen from which my visitor came. I had hunted this same bull, on and off, over a period of two years before killing it.

"If you mean the broken-horned one from the Mae-Salak," I replied, "his horns hang there over the doorway."

He turned from the fire and looked at the gaur horns that I indicated. He shook his head incredulously and said, "I would know you anywhere, O horns upon which the devils rode! Yes, those are the horns upon which my brother Eh Sha died and which I touched more than once in life." Then he stood up and walked over to the doorway without taking his eyes off the horns. "Come and look," he intoned with ritualistic fervour, "your killer is here, Eh Sha my brother, and it is now nothing but a pair of dried horns! Sleep peacefully in the hills and valleys."

Finished with this little ritual which he had spoken in his own Lisu dialect, the man smiled for the first time and sat down again by the fire. He pulled a battered pipe from his bag, reached into the fire to pick up a glowing ember with bare fingers and set it upon the bowl of the pipe. He wiped the ash from his tough, horny fingers on his soiled cloth leggings and began to puff contentedly. As the raw, powerful fumes of mountain tobacco began to permeate through the room, I turned around to exchange smiles with my wife. She did not understand Lahu, but she was fascinated by this obviously unusual visitor.

I looked at the man for a moment and thought that he would stand out anywhere, even among his own stately and proud Lisu people. A hunter's long knife in a wooden sheath, ringed with rattan bands, hung from a strap across his shoulder. Over this he carried an embroidered bag which contained all of the items he needed for travelling; important items such as pipe, tobacco, betel, some salt, a bit of bear gall and herbs. He needed no money, nor had he ever used a toothbrush or soap. It was an unnecessary extra burden to carry a blanket and a change of clothes. If friends did not feed and lodge him along the way, the jungle contained all his further needs. His hair had been cropped short at the crown and hung down in long, stringy strands along the sides and back of his head. His clothes, simple homespun cottons, reeked of smoke from campfires and mountain huts where he had huddled to dry after frequent drenchings by the rain.

He turned fierce, steady eyes towards me and betel-blackened teeth showed as he spoke again. " I am Eh Long of the three wives," he stated with considerable pride, " known among my people as a hunter and chief warrior. My dead brother, Eh Sha, was a great ' po ' (warrior) who helped me lead our people. Now that he is dead, the burden of leading my people is too heavy upon my shoulders." He paused for some time, puffing on his pipe, then continued, " I can not believe yet that the bull killed my brother because he possessed great 'ka-hta' (charms) against which bullets had no power. Even the long-fanged viper of the bamboos could not stagger him, though it bit him on the neck. But that bull though a young one, had to have powerful spirits, which had fattened on the blood of many hunters in order to kill my brother."

I was tremendously pleased with my visitor's lack of reserve. It was unusual to meet a stranger from the hills who would speak freely and easily about himself. My visitor was a hunter of very wide experience, and I valued his informative accounts, especially his intimate acquaintance with the bull of the Mae-Salak. By a strange coincidence, this same bull had been the most important one in both of our lives—he a Lisu from far in the hills, and I an

American. My visitor told me incredible things about the bull.

" This bull was no more than four years old," he began, " when it drove the spirit from Ca Maw, second headman of the Doi Uen Lahu." A total of six men had died while hunting the same bull, and Eh Long might well have been the seventh. Ca Maw had been the first victim, and the first to wound the bull with a muzzle-loader while it was yet a young herd bull. Tracking the bull into tall grass, the Lahu hunter's gun had missed fire and before he could escape, the bull had impaled its first human. " From that first wounding, the bull became wise in how to take men," my visitor said.

Going down the list of hunters one by one, Eh Long told me how each had died. All of the victims had been skilled hunters who made just one fatal mistake. The bull was not only deadly accurate with his horns, but shrewd and cunning, using deceptive tactics which experienced hunters could not always anticipate. The second victim, Ca La, a Lahu from Pi-Lu village, died because he thought he could step out of the way in time. His mistakes: underestimating the bull's speed and not " hitting the deck." A charging gaur invariably leaps over a man even though he falls flat to the ground right in the path of the charge. Their horns, curving in line with the slope of the forehead cannot reach the ground on flat places. They have the advantage, however, if a man remains standing or falls leaning against a bank or slope of a hillside.

The last four men had all been Lisu, two of them from Eh Long's village, including the last, his younger brother. Two men had died while trying to gain the lower branches of a tree, and a third Lisu had not reckoned on the bull circling from the rear while he tracked through tall grass. The last victim, Eh Sha, had not made any mistake as far as my visitor was concerned, and his case was understandably very special. The bull was by then in his eighth year, according to Eh Long's account, having killed six men in three-and-one-half years. Judging from the horns, the few rings at the base would indicate that the bull was still young and vigorous when I happened upon him a year after Eh Sha's death. Until that evening, I had not known of these victims, nor of the last one a year before. I knew only that it was a " killer bull " from what the Karen tribesmen told me, and through speculation on the broken left horn tip. It is a logical conclusion of many gaur hunters that after a bull gores a man, he tries by violent rubbing against trees and rocks to remove the scent of man, frequently breaking the tips in the process. A favourite belief of hillmen is, however, that human blood " rots " the horn tips, not through chemical action but as a punishment to the bull, brought on by guardian spirits.

As Eh Long continued his many tales concerning this particular bull, I could not help but feel that we had all been up against a very great animal. His victories over man's intelligence had not been only those six lethal times —there had been dozens of such occasions. I had been among those who were out-witted more than once. Without the power of human reasoning, the bull had survived over four years of many hunters' planned actions against him, executing superb evasive manoeuvres, charging with incredible bravery into the face of blazing guns when he deemed it the best course. His most relentless antagonists had been the two Lisu brothers.

At first it had been during the course of routine hunting for meat. The two Lisu men had decided to follow fresh gaur tracks near the very top of Sam-muen mountain. Eh Long recalled that these had been the tracks of a bull too young to be roaming away from the herd, and he had wondered why a bull in its peak breeding condition would choose the " loner's " trail. They had not known that this was the same bull which had killed Ca Maw only a few months before. " When the bull got our scent," my visitor continued, " he charged away with a snort. Eh Sha and I followed running. Suddenly, the bull wheeled in his tracks and reversed his charge, and we did look like two fools for a while, running straight at a charging bull! " The sudden switch had caught the two men completely by surprise. It had also been the first time they had encountered a gaur which used this tactic. It was a most unusual thing for a gaur to do and showed at once a versatility that was to characterise our bull of the Mae-Salak.

The two brothers were experienced and quick-thinking hunters, dropping down to the ground just as the bull reached them and leaped right over the two of them. As the bull passed, Eh Long fired into its rump. " And so I helped to make a devil out of him " he said with genuine regret.

Following the bull again on a cautious run, the brothers soon came to an open ridge just at the edge of tall grass. The ominous silence spelled trouble again, and before the men could anticipate the next charge, the bull had burst out of the tall grass to their left and came pounding down the slope at them. Eh Long recalled with an embarrassed grin, " We were the fools again for the second time in the same morning. My gun missed fire, and I was about to be gored, so I put my left hand out, grabbed the right horn by the tip and held rigidly while the bull simply swept me out of his way! Eh Sha had jumped away off the ridge and escaped with a bad cut on his heel as he landed on a sharp rock. We had to give up the chase because of that injured heel."

During the next three years, the brothers found the bull again many times. " We looked for him deliberately, like two opium addicts for their pipes, because this one had become a bad habit with us. The more we shot at him, the more we resolved to rescue the precious lead balls that he now carried. For us mountain people, lead is very hard to find. Besides, we saw him in our sleep and talked about him so much that we *had* to hunt the bull or continue as laughing stock to our people."

I estimated that the men had encountered the bull at least twenty times, following him even during the worst rains, and had shot at him more than thirty times. None of the wounds was fatal, but on one occasion when they thought they had the bull, eleven shots had been registered, many of them with serious effect, which slowed the bull down until he stopped to face them in a small ravine. Here they had run out of shot and primers. By the time they could return four days later, the bull had disappeared.

Eh Long sat cross-legged on the piece of tiger skin I had by the fireplace, gave it a disapproving glance and said, "This is a very small tiger, you should look for a bigger one!" His tale had reached the final hunt on which his brother had been with him, and my talkative visitor became reluctant to continue.

"Perhaps we can look for a big tiger together some day, but meanwhile, you must tell me the rest of your story," I replied, and was pleased to see him nod approvingly.

"One morning, Eh Sha came to my house, carrying his small newborn son and said, 'My brother, the dreams I had last night showed blood, mingled with black hairs, and a great mound of meat piled to one side. The bull is ours if we leave at once!' My own dreams had shown good omens, or so I thought, and I made haste to gather my gun, shot and powder. We two brothers left the village that morning, singing lovesongs like two young boys going out to the courting. I should have known that our happiness came from intoxicating spells of evil spirits which were calling for our souls!

"We came upon new tracks of the bull, which by now had the tips of the front hooves worn as you probably recognised yourself. This was just above the 'poang' (mineral lick) in the Mae-Salak itself. We had both loaded

up with single balls, very carefully rolled so that they
fitted tightly in the bores of our guns. Behind this, we had
five fingers* of powder, enough to kill elephant!

" *Eh Sha* and I were so used to the bull's charges by now
that it did not worry us. As I said before, I had even
touched those horns more than once! We both agreed not
to shoot on the charge so that our bullets could be carefully placed into the heart. And so we had deliberately
invited that first charge after we found the bull again,
waiting for him to become too bold and stand for an easy
shot. We were sure that we knew how to get out of the way.

" I said to my brother, ' Here he comes! ' and I remember that Eh Sha was smiling, like in a game of friendly
kick-fighting with young warriors, as he flung himself off
to my right, more concerned about what I was going to
do than for himself. Still looking back over his shoulder
at me, my brother hit a small sapling which stopped him
and held him standing for the left horn. It pierced his
chest with a crunch that I heard well and in a second he
had been borne away on that left horn. He did not even
utter a sound! " With that, my visitor leaned forward and
directed a stream of red betel juice into the fire, wiping the
dribble at the corner of his mouth with his fingers, then
rubbing his fingers over his leggings. Ochre stains marked
the sides of both leggings from long practice of this habit.
I pictured the man sitting by another fire over a year
before, gazing with the same expression into the flames,
while beside him lay the still form of his brother under
banana leaves which sheltered the broken warrior from
the light drizzle. Eh Long had carried the corpse all the

---

* Hillmen measure powder charges in their muzzle-loaders by placing
fingers horizontally alongside the protruding ramrods at the muzzles.
The tamped powder at " three fingers " is a usual load for the average,
roughly ·50-calibre guns. " Five fingers " indicate a maximum load,
often resulting in blown barrels. The black powder is home-made, using
saltpetre (Potassium nitrate) from bat guano which hillmen process
themselves.

way back to the village so that many pigs could be killed for the sacrifice at the grave, and had erected a great mound over the grave upon which was placed tall clumps of thatch-grass—the " hair " by which his brother's soul could be lifted by unseen spirits for the long and complicated journey to the warriors' heaven.

Concluding his story, he said, " I was like a madman after that, remembering neither to sleep nor to eat, and following the bull when I should have been tending the opium fields. My two younger wives nearly left me, having run off for a time with young warriors who could better attend them. By harvest time, I was so weary from chasing the bull that I remained at home while you came up into the Mae-Salak, and because you did not have a madman's desire for vengeance, the spirits gave you those horns. I would have chopped them in small pieces, and left the meat to rot and feed the dogs of the jungle! "

An earlier, coincidental meeting with this man might well have occurred while I had been on the trail of the same bull. I recalled that on a number of occasions, I had seen his barefoot tracks along the streams and in the tracks of the bull. These my Lahu companions and I had commented on as possibly belonging to the primitive Phi-Tong-Luang,* for we never saw Eh Long's camps, and it did not seem likely that any other tribe would be so bold as to hunt alone in the Mae-Salak.

Eh Long sat silently, nodding his head and grunting occasionally in an understanding way, as I tried to go through the various episodes of my own hunting for the bull before midnight rolled around. When I had completed my tale, we finished the last two cups of green tea and I

---

* " Spirits of the Yellow Leaf," a tribe (or tribes) which have possibly retrogressed to a strictly jungle economy, using spears for hunting and as religious symbols to be worshipped. Their usual roving areas are to the east, on the Thai-Laos border, but a band or two apparently did roam the Doi Uen-Mae Taeng section according to Lisu and Lahu hunters who had seen them.

showed my visitor to a small " guest house " which had been made specially for hillmen who came to stay the night at my place in Chiengmai. I came back into the house, shivering from the cold, and looked up at the horns over the doorway again. It had been my prize trophy without Eh Long's detailed revelations, but it was now even more meaningful to me. Only two months before, we had returned from the Mae-Salak with the horns, and the memories were vivid, going back two years when I first encountered the bull of the Mae-Salak, or " dish-toes " as we came to know him.

We had come into the Mae-Salak quite by chance that first time. With six Lahus, I had gone into the headwaters of the Mae Taeng river, in the north of Chiengmai province approaching from a point ninety kilometres north on the Chiengmai-Fang road. For five days, we followed the river southwards, " looking over new country " as the men called it, until we came to the Karen village of Muang Khawng. That evening, the headman of the main village, called respectfully by the Shan title of *pu-hing,* invited me to come to his house for a sip of new home-made rice *lao.* He was a jolly old boy, a typically tattooed Shan of the old school, with magnificent moustache and a flaring pink turban. Few visitors from the world beyond came to visit his quaint little village since some thirty years before when British teak companies had been active along the Mae Taeng. I was treated like a member of the old British Raj, and my host did not seem to realise that this was not Burma, from whence he had come twenty years earlier, and that I was an American non-official. Pretty, curvaceous Shan girls served tea and *lao,* humbly observing the formalities of crawling around on hands and knees while catering refreshments to seated males. My host was the picture of a Shan *Sawbwa* (prince), using the flowery official language with relish, most of which I could not understand, much less Big Pig and New Soul who spoke some Shan—atrociously.

" I am glad that (flowery word) . . . came to (flowery words) . . . and we (flowery words) . . . to be in the business of teak work which (flowery words) . . . and (more flowery words) . . . etc." I thought I had the point, however, and tried to explain to the headman that I was not inspecting teak forests. This he did not understand until he had concluded a well-prepared speech, and because New Soul was rudely interrupting with gestures of shooting a gun. The Chief looked shocked and said, " The Japanese? "

" Much worse," I said in a combination of Shan and Muang, " Lahus—six Lahus and a ' Farang '*! " He looked mortified until I said, "We have come to hunt, *ying sadt,* while we get acquainted with what is new country to us."

The old man tossed his head back and cackled with delight, then repaired the loop of turban that had been loosed. "Ah yes! The *chao wohn* (Assistant Superintendent) comes to *yeu sadt!* " He corrected my dialectic difference, with an insistence that I should speak strictly Shan. Then New Soul asked a question concerning the girls, with his mutilated, clipped, rude Shan expression, without final consonants, which the old man fortunately could not understand. I changed this quickly into, " We were wondering what kind of orchid that girl wears in her hair? " and gave New Soul a searing look.

" Ah! That is the *dawk nam phueng.* Have you never seen them before? "

" No," I lied, thinking that I had at least fifty nests of the common yellow Dendrobium at my home. " Now, if the *pu hing* will be so kind, would he speak of the hunting to be found in this area? "

The *pu hing,* already happy on the strong *lao* before we had come, became comically serious, patting his luxuri-

---

* *Farang,* a local idiom for any Caucasian foreigner.

ous moustaches and assuming the dignified countenance of one who is about to announce grand matters of state. The jungles in his jurisdictional area, he said, contained *everything*. We were most welcomed to hunt, of course, but did we realise that there were terrible *phi* (spirits) in the jungles that could even kill us? Why, there was Sang Noi, his nephew, who had been enticed by a *phi kong koi*, which sang a lovely lovesong and tinkled bells, and even appeared as a beautiful maiden, to lure him into a forest clearing where he suddenly found a great king cobra, head raised about to attack him. " And somewhere up on the stream which they call the *Mae-Salak*, there are ancient ruins of Wa temples, containing fortunes in gold and silver, but these are guarded by spirits in the form of huge serpents, and whoever touches the treasures will fall down at once and die of nose-bleeding! "

We thanked the *pu hing* for his hospitality, assured him that we would never bother the spirits of the jungles and left his house to find out directions from the Karens for a casual reconnaissance of the Mae-Salak. The possibility of locating any Wa ruins was of much interest to me, as friends in the Siam Society had asked me particularly to be on the watch for just such traces of the ancient Wa, who were believed to have lived in northern Thailand some two thousand years ago. There was also the promise that we would be in excellent big game country.

While we discussed directions in a smoke-filled Karen house by the rushing rapids of the Mae Taeng, a commotion on the rickety porch announced the arrival of " Bui-bui," a man who was most valuable in this and subsequent visits to this area. Freshly wounded by a glancing blow from his axe while chopping wood, one of the most cheerful persons I have met came limping and laughing into the room. He was naked except for a skimpy waist cloth and covered with an amazing affliction of warts—absolutely covered from face to feet. He had a wad of leaves pressed against a two-inch-long gash in his shin, tied in place with string, and the blood continued flowing crimson down to his ankle. "Ai-yo! *Pai nai ma?*" he half yelled, as though he had known me for years.

He sat down next to me by the hearth, squinted in the dim light to see what I looked like, then leaned over to scrape the blood off his leg with a long knife, edge perpendicular to the trickle of blood. He wiped this on a stick of firewood, still smiling, then turned again to me. "I am Bui-bui," he said with another disarming smile that showed strong, white teeth. The man may have had a number of vices, but betel-chewing was not one of them.

"Your people have been telling me about you," I replied, "and from what I've heard, I hope you will join me tomorrow for a few days of hunting in the Mae-Salak."

Bui-bui's eyes brightened at once, "Ai-yo! You should have arrived just three days ago and gone with me up to the big *poang*. I came upon eleven head of *kating* (gaur) and wished that I had a herd of cattle like that! If you can be ready before the cocks crow, we will start, and I will show you the best way to the Mae-Salak. Pho-hto-hto-hto! It is a place for a hunter!"

I could see Big Pig, New Soul and Stud Bull smiling, and knew that they liked this mountain man at once. He was a S'kaw Karen,* a tribe to which the Lahu have always felt a close ethnic affiliation, although this is very doubtful considering the vast differences in the two languages.

When he had said, "before the cocks crow," Bui-bui had meant it. I looked at my watch after Stud Bull woke me and announced that Bui-bui had come. It was just 2.30 a.m. I heard the now familiar "Ho-ha-ha-ha," followed by rapid dialogue in Karen. I was surprised to see that one of

---

* All of the numerous Karen tribes are of the same Tibeto-Burman race as are the Lahu, Lisu and Akha. Karens are better known as a group in Burma which have stoutly resisted amalgamation with the Union since its independence from the British. They are represented in Thailand by scattered groups on the western borders.

my Lahu boys, Solid Log, sat near Bui-bui, conversing in Karen with expert command of the difficult tongue. He had mentioned very modestly that he could speak some Karen, and I had assumed that that meant a few basic words. I still had a lot to learn about my Lahu companions.

" Teh K'u, you old *Yang-keu-leu!* Where did you learn to speak the language? " I enquired of Solid Log as I struggled out of my sleeping bag.

" Ah, Jaw Maw, that is a long story. I served with them during the fight against the ' Japa ' (Japanese)." I made a note of that and planned to ask him sometime about his experiences. They proved to be as interesting as I had expected: wounded twice by mortars, killed four Japanese at night with a knife, and reached Rangoon and Moulmein.

A quarter moon gave me just enough light to see the slippery trail, still wet from the monsoons which had not quite ended. Three hours later, as the faint glow of dawn became recognisable, we had passed the last small rice field and the limits of ranging for village buffaloes. I bent down low and made out imprints of a large tiger which had braced front feet heavily in the sand while it drank from a small pool of water. The sight, as always, sent a thrill through me. Bui-bui watched my excited inspection and chuckled. " One time, I saw him here, just at this same time of day, and you can imagine, *nai,* that I did not feel too brave, being all alone! "

" *Shoot* at him! We Karens do not even like to *talk* about tigers, for fear that the spirits will send them into the buffaloes. You talk about them enough, *nai,* and you will surely see one! "

" Keep talking about tigers, my brothers! " I hoped with a passion that we might see one, preferably when the light got better, and hopped across the creek after Bui-bui.

At mid-morning, we stopped to cook a meal of rice and

fish which the boys caught with bare hands from a stream. When we had finished, clouds rolled up from the west and thunder rumbled briefly before a strong downpour had us all huddled under sheets of plastic. It did not last long, but an annoying drizzle continued as we trudged up a long slope going west. To the south of this the Mae-Salak could be heard where it cascaded over several ledges down in the gorge. Our destination was the headwaters, another day's climb beyond the pine forests that were typical of this section. When we made camp for the night, the drizzle had stopped and the sky showed blue through several gaps in the fleecy cumulus clouds above the grey mist. It seemed that we had climbed much higher into the mountains than the 4,000 feet of actual elevation at that point. New Soul used a single ·22 bullet to bring in a large male leaf monkey, our meat for the evening.

Before we reached the cave above the *poang* the next morning, Bui-bui knelt down by some tracks implanted in old elephant skid marks near a small creek. He turned to me and said, " *Nai,* this is the big bull ' kating ' that I mentioned last night. It travels alone and I have been charged by it twice, and it is much bigger than you might guess from the tracks. See how the front hooves are short at the tips—worn from much climbing in the rocky places."

I was looking at the tracks of " Dish-toes," the bull which had by then, unknown to any of us, killed five men already. A year later, Eh Sha was to die just two hundred yards down the hill from where we stood. Bui-bui had seen it several times during the few months preceding our visit and had shot at it twice, when he had been charged. " It did not appear to even notice the bullets," he exclaimed shaking his head sadly, then inspecting his old muzzle-loader's rust-pitted bore. " If I had that ' too-expensive-kind ' gun you carry, he would have died where he stood! " I grinned back at him and handed him my old Springfield ·30/06, purchased second-hand from a swap shop in Pasadena for a price not much above what he paid in hard-earned silver for his own musket. He rubbed loving hands over the rifle for the tenth time since I had met him. He had never seen such an " expensive " weapon, and to think that it could shoot from one side of the valley and kill a sambar on the other side! A man would gladly trade his wife, children, pigs, chickens and three buffaloes for such a gun.

We had settled into " Bui-bui's cave " when the rain came. It was night—so pitch dark at 5.30 p.m. that you could not see your hand in front of your face. The leeches had also been at their aggressive worst, so men sat around the warming fires, scraping them off by the dozens from their legs with knives, and tossing the plump, blood-filled bodies into the flames. New Soul had a good, filthy joke at the tip of his tongue and was trying to get attention away from Big Pig's colourful swearing, when I saw his face suddenly twist into a grimace of pain. His left foot came up briefly and his heel thudded down upon something that crunched. I saw the tail of the centipede twitch back and forth under his grinding heel. " May the thunder and lightening take you, plague-stricken eater of snakes' carcass! " He kicked the mangled creature into the fire and sat gripping his ankle. From many such experiences, Big Pig calmly pulled his razor-sharp skinning knife and made two neat incisions into the two dots marking the " fang " punctures. Although degrading for a man to place lips upon another's foot, Big Pig would have used his mouth to remove as much of the venom as possible. But I had already assembled my small suction pump from the snake-bite kit and we used that instead. I cleaned the wound later and disinfected it and the operation was so successful that New Soul slept well that night. Untreated, he might not have walked for two or three days.

We awoke to a fresh, dripping dawn, full of earthy fragrance and the sounds of many birds. Muddied by the violent rains during the night, the stream flowed wildly over the large boulders, swollen to the height of the willows on the opposite bank. From the mouth of the cave, I watched hypertense chipmunks scurrying along the wet branches, exploring and inspecting minute details in the bark. Over the top of stately bamboos, I could see a tall deadwood, its uppermost branch supporting a serpent eagle, feathers ruffled in the morning, preening. Different troops of gibbons tried each to out-do the other in a whooping contest up and down the ravine, blending their song in a wild din.

About three hours later, when he had climbed over the top of the ridge behind the cave and come into a grass-covered flat near the head of the left fork of the stream, I stood with Bui-bui and Big Pig, squinting against the sun at a dark mass in low bamboos. I raised my rifle as it moved, very suddenly, and with a great crashing the big bull was gone. Without a word, the three of us made our way across the grass as fast as we could, picked up the dish-toed tracks and followed it down through the bamboos. My first contact with the big bull ended in near-disaster for at least one of us. He led us first across a small stream and while we traversed the steep bank, he came down upon us with a blasting snort. Big Pig slid behind a tree, Bui-bui fell flat to the right of the charge, and I flopped sidewise into sting-nettle on the left. The bull bounded through us like a run-away steamroller. We were all armed, primed to shoot. Nobody shot. Nobody had time. Two days later, we still had not caught up with the bull and abandoned the first attempt in favour of a big stag *sambar* which I got near our third camp.

We planned to come back another time to look for the " lost Wa temples " (which we never found) and to follow the bull again. That had been almost two years to the day before the final attempt, the sixth of my Mae-Salak expeditions.

To the best of my recollection and during the course of twenty-two days of actual tracking, I followed those dish-toed tracks over approximately 130 miles, was charged four times by the same animal, and saw him nine times. I had tried several other elusive bull gaur in other places, and bagged them successfully in between the Mae-Salak trips. This area, however, proved most fruitful as far as other big game went. Every trip produced at least bear, leopard, *sambar*, boar, or wild goat. By the 8th of November, 1958, we had made the trip often enough and had learned something about time-saving routes and which man carried just what. We were at the *poang* below the cave camp early in the morning, just three days after leaving Chiengmai, ninety kilometres away over the hills.

My usual gang was with me: Big Pig, Little Pig, Stud Bull, New Soul, Solid Log, Bui-bui and his young nephew, Ta-mu. The evening before, at "*Nga peh pa*" (Plenty fish camp), I made a prediction which I had done many times before: "Tomorrow at 7 o'clock, we arrive at *poang*. Big bull is eating at *poang*. We start skinning him at fifteen minutes after seven! The response, as usual, was good hearty laughter. There was one change that might have had a bearing upon the luck—Little Pig saw not three, but five naked maidens in his dream the night before! He said that this was positively auspicious this time. The vote showed three in favour, three against and two undecided. We might or might not be lucky.

As a result of a bad experience while shooting a banteng bull (wild red cattle) a year before, I now carried a heavier rifle in addition to the Springfield. This was a new Winchester ·375 Magnum. When Bui-bui saw it for the first time, he was speechless with awe. "The *most* expensive gun in the world," he called it, "So powerful that it could cause the worst devils to retreat." It did have certain merits over the ·30/06 when it came to gaur and banteng.

With only one break en route, we arrived at the over-

66

hang above the *poang* at five minutes to seven, on schedule according to my prediction. But there was no bull gaur standing in the mineral lick. Big Pig and I stalked down to the main deposit of clay which had been gouged and licked by numerous big game including elephant, and saw the dish-toed tracks fresh on the trampled flat. He had moved to the right and stood under a fig tree, urinated there and then crossed the stream. Big Pig whistled like a quail, the signal for the men behind to remain in place and very quiet. I checked the heavy Model 70, released the safety and moved out ahead of Big Pig along the wet tracks. The ·375 felt heavy and awkward in my hand, but it was re-assuring to have a suitable calibre of rifle for so tough a customer as " Dish-toes." I gripped it tightly, and checked the safety again, then ducked carefully under the low hang-ing bamboos on the other side of the stream. The wind was coming from my right, going downstream—so far so good. The time: 7.10 when the bull ought to be grazing carelessly in the first patch of grass that he found. Big Pig and I *knew* he would be just fifty yards above us on the small clearing which we had passed many times before. He should be standing in the middle of the patch where there were few burr plants to annoy him. I peeked slowly through the last canopy of bamboos and saw the bull, standing in plain view for the first time. It had always been a fleeting glimpse every other time before that, and I could hardly believe my luck. It was the culmination of much more than ten minutes of tracking from the *poang*. I had hoped for such a meeting for hundreds of hours, saw him in this stance as many times in my mind's eye, and now I felt a strange reluctance to complete what I had sweated for hundreds of miles to do.

Big Pig, just behind me, saw the bull from a more obscured angle. He said later that he could not understand my moment's hesitation. I was jolted from my awed gaze when I realised that the bull had raised his head and was looking squarely in my direction. He was quartered away, looking back around his right shoulder, standing motionless. He had either gotten my scent, heard my heart beating, or had fantastic premonition. From the thirty-odd yards, I knew that I could not miss, and stepped out of the bamboos, giving him a good look at me while I raised the rifle, took quick aim at the heart and fired just as he lurched into a turn. I saw hair flick, just high and behind a correct line to the heart which lay low in the chest. I felt momentary defeat again as the huge beast lined up straight for me and began increasing in size as he neared. He did not appear to feel the bullet, as Bui-bui had said of his two shots. I worked a second round into the chamber with what seemed like great difficulty; the bolt was longer and stiffer than that of my Springfield. With a grunt, Big Pig had taken cover to my right and I was trying to take aim again.

Almost too late, I stepped aside, let the bull pass me and the line of aim which would have included Big Pig's position, then I squeezed the trigger again, rifle at my hip. I saw the bullet strike sickeningly high in the gut. When his head had been just opposite to me, he had dipped his head low in an effort to hook me with his horn, blowing and snorting. I noticed later that a quantity of bubbly "lung wound" blood had splattered across the front of my khaki shirt. Then he stopped abruptly ten yards below me and turned to face me again. To me, just then, he was the picture of the bravest of the brave bulls. He would have given it one more good try, though mortally wounded, even *uphill*. The third of my 300-grain bullets crashed into the front of the great, broad chest, driving down above the brisket into the heart. The long chase was over, and I cheered loudly, in all honesty, for that magnificent animal. Had I known the full story, the other men's experiences and deaths, and how he had also resisted them, I think I would have wept. For me, he was not only the largest of many gaur I had encountered, he was certainly the most unforgettable.

In a little while, the men were all gathered around the bull which lay on its left side, exposing all three of my bullet strikes. Bui-bui was more interested in inspecting my rifle again, stroking it like some magic wand, muttering strange words in Karen to himself. The bull's withers rested against a tree, and from a point up on the trunk, I measured straight across to the heel of the front hoof. It was exactly six-and-one-half feet. I could only guess at the body weight. Give or take a few hundred pounds, I was probably not too far off at 3,000 pounds liveweight. The horns, with the broken left tip, were not meant for this huge individual, and they looked puny in comparison to the body. Only the broad spread of the forehead distinguishes it from my other trophies.

We sat around, trying to decide how to begin the all-day task of carving and preparing the ton of meat. As though on cue, it began to rain. I stood up and walked over to Big Pig who had not bothered to take cover, still looking at the great bull before us, and I knew that he too was thinking of the long trail we had taken after this animal. He turned to me and said, " Jaw Maw, even the gods respected this one, but their tears are of joy for us, so let them soak us! "

CHAPTER FOUR

Leopards that Crossed the Trail

" Po ui po cheu hpeh ga k'o la bvuh ta he nyi-o."
" If a great warrior you would be, watch the leopards and learn."

I WOKE with a start, and found that the nightmare I had experienced was real. My face and arms *were burning up!* Worse yet, when I wiped my hand across my face, I had developed thousands of scales where skin used to be, and this horror spread immediately to my hand. I jerked up to a sitting position and yelled, " Help! "

The burning, stinging sensation was unbearable and when I rubbed my eyes, I became blinded, driven to further desperation. Helpless, I tumbled from my sleeping bag, screamed louder and became more panic-stricken as the burning invaded my mouth. Then I felt strong hands gripping me and a voice that I hardly recognised saying, " Wait! Wait! Jaw Maw! Hold still for a moment! " A flashlight flicked on my face and a rough cloth was being used to wipe it. The voice continued to reassure me, but I was nearly driven to insanity—sure that I would yet die. Had I been alone, I might have stumbled madly about, smashing into jagged rocks behind the camp, or impaled myself on a sharp bamboo stake.

"A few hundred do not hurt, but ten thousand do. Jaw Maw is to be pitied," Big Pig was saying as he continued to wipe at my face and arms vigorously with the rough turban. The sour, acidic smell of the countless mashed bodies of wood termites stung my nose and my eyes. I could

70

only groan and submit to the helping hands, very grateful for each word of reassurance. I knew what had happened now, but the pain was still intense from thousands of imbedded heads, detached from bodies and still holding on tenaciously. I was trembling in a cold sweat as Big Pig's knife began systematically to shave my nose, lips, eyelids and other parts. The process of coming back from what seemed the brink of death was difficult, slow and torturous. I thanked God for my good companions.

When I was somewhat rational again, I saw men busying themselves around the fire which had been built up to blazing flames. My sleeping bag was being immersed briefly in and out of the flames to singe off masses of swarming termites. Then I saw my new leather boots singed free of the damnable insects. What had been smooth leather before, had been transformed—in the course of probably no more than fifteen minutes—into a suede. Given another fifteen minutes, I might not have had boots, gun slings, rucksack and several other items of gear. The jungle termite, much more voracious than his relations which specialise in wood houses, eats everything, stops at nothing, and has an abominable odour when smashed. A bluish stain remains on all surfaces across which they have been wiped. In his own right, this smallest of jungle creatures is among the most fearsome customers to meet.

Later, as we sat about the fire while I dabbed my washed face with alcohol, Big Pig grinned at me across the fire. " There's a Lahu saying, ' *Pu wu haw taw a g'a* (Termites can't stop an elephant). Do you agree? "

"As far as I am concerned, termites can stop anything! They stopped me tonight, and did I not stop the big bull elephant on Doi Vieng? " We had a good laugh together at the ridiculous logic and I was made well again. It was just past four o'clock in the morning; we would finish the night around the fragrant smell of pine logs which blazed in the fire, sip green tea and listen to the early morning sounds of the jungle.

The Mae Suet, a hundred kilometres to the south of Chiengmai, was new country to us. We had made a wrong turn at the last Karen village, so that we were a day's hike away from the valley we intended to visit. Just one mistake like that in this country, we learned, could be worse than taking a wrong ridge in the *yeh* that we all were more at home in. There you could always depend on finding good water in any of the numerous valleys. Here, the country was for many miles at a stretch, open, sparse forestland on rocky and bone-dry terrain, especially during the dry season from January to May. But beyond this rolling region, green mountains beckoned, and we had been told—quite falsely—that even rhinos were to be found in those mountains. That had been a typical exaggeration of a plainsman, a sometime hunter who could see " fifty elephant when five deer stood together," as Big Pig said with scorn. Few men had ventured into those mountains besides the Meo and Shelleh who lived far to the south. They might have given us better directions and told us where the red cattle ranged. But it was our pleasure to follow the nose, camping whenever it got dark and finding out for ourselves.

We had not yet reached good game country and to continue in a direct course to the mountains might bring us into serious situations for water. So we moved out the next morning, doubling back for a few miles then cutting straight across a wide range to the south. This brought us out into an active stream, the real Mae Suet, which wound up through rising mountains to the northwest. I was surprised to find a well-used trail going up its left bank, and still more surprised to find a Karen village, or what had been a village, about a mile upstream.

An old Karen man and two young women were just coming from the abandoned village, starting down the trail in our direction. They seemed to be the last people leaving, having collected various odds and ends left behind, which they thought were worth salvaging. I greeted them and asked them why they were moving. The old man took a short, curved silver pipe out of his mouth and gave me a toothless grin, simply nodding his head in the affirmative. " But why? " I asked again.

As though an answer to this question should first be rewarded, he chomped his gums together for a moment, looking suspiciously at me, then said, " Old Uncle is needing medicine for strength."

I had one for him right from my shirt pocket—a cough drop wrapped up like a toffee. His eyes lit up—" Just one more! " He was awarded a second cough drop and I waited a few minutes for him to get started with the first. Meanwhile the two girls kept puffing on their pipes, staring at me, unblinking, like two terrified does.

" We move because bad spirits tax us heavily in this place," the old man finally managed with great difficulty in Muang. " It is many things—partly from the promiscuity of our young people, and partly because too many souls have fled the bodies of our people."

I nodded, trying to look very sage, and asked him what " evil spirits " we should watch out for up the stream.

" They are in the form of leopard," he said, " which come down from the hills to take away our cattle and pigs to punish our wrong doings! "

" Leopards! Do you have many in this area? "

" You will believe that there are many if you are foolish enough to hunt in the Mae Suet! " He had had enough and motioned to the two girls to follow him down the trail. They were handsomely proportioned girls dressed in the one-piece gowns of the unmarried. Solid Log, who could speak S'kaw Karen, said something to them that I could guess was more than ladies usually stand for. The girls kept right on walking and spat to one side of the trail in a token of disdain. He said something more, with a sort of purring in the last words and stopped the girls in their tracks. Their sullen faces changed as they turned to face him fully, and in their own way, the smiles were beautiful. Instead of flashing white teeth, the betel stains had a kind of ebony attractiveness, exactly matching the raven hair. It was somehow becoming to these jungle people.

An hour's travel upstream had us well into the steep-walled canyons which line the upper portions of this valley. Here we found tracks of leopard at several places in the sand, all of them old, indicating that the Karens had moved their livestock a good week before and discouraged further hunting in the area. We dismissed any possibilities of meeting leopard along the stream and turned to the business of making tracks towards the mountains far up the valley.

Near the headwaters, the barren ridges rose sharply on both banks and the stream flowed gently through the gorge, forming numerous pools among great boulders, green-covered with algae. Huge *mai huak* bamboos towered over the stream from foot-thick bases and the fallen leaves covered the stream-bed with a golden carpet. On the right side of a sharp bend in the stream, we paused to catch our breath, resting on a large, flat boulder. It was nearly noon and time that we stopped to make our first meal of the day which we usually had at around ten o'clock. For this reason we sat only a few minutes then moved on to find a suitable spot by the stream. We had no sooner got to our feet when the unmistakable sawing coughs of a leopard came echoing down the canyon. I looked back at Big Pig and New Soul. They were just as surprised as I was to hear a leopard's call at high noon. There had been no tracks on the sand to show that it had gone upstream just ahead of us, so it must be coming down towards us. I slipped off my kit bag and stepped off up the stream, hopping from boulder to boulder, while the rest of the men remained behind.

When I reached the next big bend, I released the safety lever of my Springfield and slowly came around a rocky bank. The calls came again from about a hundred yards, beyond another bend. I could still see the men behind me as I climbed on a large boulder and squatted down, waiting for the leopard to come down the stream. It would be as easy as that to get another fine skin, and judging from the full, rich voice, it *must* be a big male. A slight breeze came from upstream and cooled my face; I smiled to myself that everything was just right; no long night's waiting for this one!

I gave the leopard ten minutes for a slow, casual prowl down the stream, then raised the rifle, aiming at the exact spot on the right bank from which he should appear. There were no more calls and there appeared no leopard. All was a deathly silence. Still aiming my rifle from my squatting position, I frowned and wondered what was keeping the big cat. Then I realised that the leopard had probably found a shady spot in which to stretch out for a nap. Actually, there was no definite reason to believe that the leopard was moving down the stream in the heat of the day; it was more likely that he had been doing his calling from the same place. There was only one thing to do—*bring him out.* To stalk him in that situation would have been hopeless. On the other hand, my simple method of decoying would have the leopard stalking me, out of sheer curiosity and without serious effort to conceal himself, while I could wait in readiness. So I placed the palm of my hand to my mouth and sucked through puckered lips, making a squealing sound like a rabbit in distress.

After about two minutes of this periodic squealing, and just when I thought the leopard was too far away to hear me, he came bounding around the bend like a big, playful kitten. He saw me at once as I moved my right hand to the trigger and took aim. Without stopping, he turned sharply to his left and leaped into the tall ferns. My shot crashed into the area where his head and neck should have been inside the ferns. There was a loud cough, followed by throaty growling, then the leopard sprang back onto the open sandspit and rose on his haunches, wiping at his face with both paws. I lowered the rifle, certain that I had hit him in the throat and that the leopard was thrashing in death. It seemed that there was no need to rip up the beautiful skin with another shot. How wrong I was! Suddenly he leaped again, in the same direction, for the same ferns, and I fired again repeating just what I had done before. This time there was a different kind of growling, more intense and higher-pitched, and he did not come out of the ferns. I heard the leopard crashing away up the side of the stream through low bushes, leaving me to stand peering from the rock, feeling absolutely rotten.

In about five or six seconds I had sent two 180-grain bullets at a big male leopard while it moved rapidly, obscured from view, behind obstructions that could deflect my rounds, and made two of my worst mistakes in quick succession. I deserved to feel rotten, and later I probably deserved the scare of my life as punishment for poor judgement. To say the least, I had bungled things very badly. Big Pig reached me; carrying my 12-gauge double shotgun and smiling broadly he asked me if I had killed the leopard. I told him what had happened and he lost the expectant smile.

Taking the 12-gauge, I checked both barrels to see that they contained " oo " buckshot. Big Pig gave me two more rounds and these I put in my right pocket. I had every intention of trying to redeem myself from the disgrace that I was heaping upon my good record. The least I could do was to keep the other men out of a quarrel that I had been responsible for. So I told Big Pig to take my rifle and remain well behind me, knowing that I might have to shoot in any direction when I came upon the leopard again.

I could be sure of one thing—the leopard would come charging. The shotgun was my best weapon now.

Big Pig helped me find the blood trail and together we learned that one of my bullets had struck a rock just in front of the leopard's face. This had probably splattered into his face the first time and might not have been too serious. My second shot had gone lower and more to the left, closer to the leopard's body. I started out after a thin blood trail which soon became an occasional drop. About ten yards from the first blood, I found a chip of bone on a leaf which did not make me feel any better. It had come from the joint of a limb; I assumed it to be from the elbow. I was tracking a wounded leopard alone now, and from what I knew about wounded leopards, my wheels were as good as set on collision course. I moved very slowly, watching and listening with senses strained, trying to keep at least ten yards between myself and any suspicious-looking thickets. It is probably accurate to say that most shooters, myself included, are not fast enough in their reactions to aim and fire at a leopard springing out from ten yards. Down a slight grade, this is simply a single good leap for him. A man is almost better off doing the spear trick— allowing the big cat to impale himself upon a braced spear as many of the hilltribes do.

How badly the leopard had been wounded I did not know, but judging from the long leaps over the fallen bamboo leaves, it seemed that he was having no serious difficulties. He kept to the same side of the stream for about seventy-five yards then crossed. The water was red in a small pool where he had lain for a few minutes, cooling the fresh wounds. My interest was taken enough while studying the reddened pool that I became careless, and might well have had a snarling leopard on me. The leopard had crossed the stream and gone into a dense thorn thicket about five yards on the other bank. This was where I should have used much better judgement, for had he been in the thorns, he could have reached me easily in one leap. I told myself that this was the way men got killed following leopards, even the careful ones. It was time I stopped making mistakes.

I got back quickly to the left bank again, took a better grip of my nerves and decided that I would skirt the thorn bushes from upstream, with a very strong feeling that the leopard was even then lying just inside. My efforts took about ten minutes, and only made me lose the blood trail. I squatted just above the thorns where I could peer under them and scan the steep slope to my right. Sweat poured from my face and I felt my heart pounding even though I had moved so slowly that there had been no physical exertion. About two stanzas of some song that I knew vaguely kept going through my head, repeated over and over. It was a dead silence in which I thought I should wait for as long as necessary until the leopard broke it by shifting position or by letting out a grunt. Surely he could not remain motionless for long with wounds to trouble him.

I waited for ten minutes then began to have doubts that the leopard could still be near. I moved cautiously to where I thought he might have come out of the thorns to either continue up the stream, or climb up into the rocky hillside. There was no sign of a bleeding animal having passed through, and the only trees that he might have climbed were small saplings under the tall bamboos. He had not left the ground, I was sure. I squatted once more, taking several minutes to study the slope rising above me. It occurred to me then that the leopard must surely be up among the rocks and bamboo clumps because there were many good hiding places there. I tried squealing again, hoping that this might bring out a growl. The same silence continued. Then I heard a subtle whistle from across the stream, just where I had left the blood trail. I whistled back, then in a low voice told Big Pig that I had lost the trail. I never finished my sentence, and swung round to face an eruption that was as big as a volcano to me just then—more so because I was tensed for it.

The sound is hard to describe. It was a combination of quickly inhaled-exhaled grunts, coughs, and a hoarse spitting. The leopard might have emitted the first coughs right after leaving his position behind a flat rock. What I saw was a flashing blur of brown, the spots blending unrecognisably with the yellow fur. His rasping growls accentuated the fury that was behind the attack and reverberated through the valley with a stunning effect. Clutched by a terrified wonder at the suddenness of the attack, and at the unbelievable speed with which the animal was sailing down the slope, I raised my shotgun and was shooting without being able to recall any command of my faculties to do so. Then I was shooting the other barrel and instinctively leaping out of the way of the flying body. It landed with a great thud just where I had been standing, and might well have—as I expected it to do—twisted to one side and jumped on me. But somehow, my aim had been true, and somehow I *had aimed*.

This, the angriest of leopards that I had encountered, had been sporting enough to give me twenty-five yards. Five yards less and he might have won. The force of his crash, even if he had been mortally hit, would have crushed me to the ground. I am sure that he covered the distance in less than three seconds. One second I lost in the initial focusing of sight and senses to the moving animal. I probably aimed and shot within one-and-a-half seconds and went for dear life in the remaining half-second. With a half-second more, he would have won as far as I was concerned, but not totally, I am convinced. What happened just afterwards will remain with me always.

With a great shout, the man who would have killed the leopard had I not done so, came leaping through the thorns.

He moved faster than any human being I have seen going through that sort of brush, and in his hand he held his long knife instead of my rifle. Big Pig was magnificent. I knew then that I had a great and loyal friend who had come to what he thought was my rescue with the urgency of a true comrade. His joy at seeing me unharmed was so genuine that my heart warmed to this brother of the hunt with a new confidence and the kind of fondness that I have rarely felt for a friend. Blood dripped from the terrible thorn rips on his face and ears, the scars from which would always remain to remind us both of the incident. In his hand was his famous *Hpa-leang* blade which he had used in combat more than once, and against which I doubt the leopard could have won.

" I heard the growls," he fairly shouted, breathing very hard, " then a shot and more growling. My spirit fled because I thought that you were by then under the leopard's claws!" He paused for breath, then laughed, " It is a happy ending just the same, Jaw Maw!"

He called the boys behind, and we went to see what had happened to the leopard from the first contact to the last. My first shot, ricocheting on the rock, had thrown pieces of lead into the leopard's face, one of them severing a canine tooth. The second shot had hit the right elbow at the tip of the joint, ripping the skin and chipping the bone, but without disabling him. Both of my buckshot loads from the shotgun had hit him flush in the chest, the last from so close that the felt wads were embedded in the single gaping wound. He was in mid-air when my last round was fired, striking him between extended front legs low in the heavy chest. Measured " between the pegs " he was seven feet four-and-one-half inches from tip of nose to tip of tail, only one inch shorter, though more massive, than the largest leopard in my life. He was a beautiful male in prime condition, and I was able to patch up the bad rips in the skin for one of my most treasured trophies.

When the other men arrived, we made camp at the stream. Instead of the banteng steaks that we had hoped for, we had curried leopard. I had spent the rest of the day dressing out the skin, carefully skinning out the lips, eyelids, ears, and scraping all of the thick skin as thin as possible before applying salt and alum. By the end of the day, I had had to go meticulously over my own skin, removing hundreds of ticks that had evacuated the leopard and found new pastures. The Mae Suet leopard proved to be a champion host for both ticks and chiggers.

At dusk, the job of dressing the skin still incomplete, a series of leopard calls came from the ridge above and to the right of our camp. We listened for a while to the female, looking for the mate I had killed, as she went along the top of the gorge, crossed about a quarter of a mile down the stream and came back up the opposite edge. I left the skin in Little Pig's care and picked up my shotgun and flashlight. About two hundred yards down the stream below our camp I chose a place to intercept her, using another " dirty trick " to obtain another skin that might bring a good price. I had saved the leopard's testicles which I tossed up the canyon wall near to where I thought she might soon be passing. Then I sat down on a rock to wait and my thoughts went back to many leopards that had crossed the trail.

No two experiences had been the same or even similar. I had just gone through my most thrilling encounter with a charging leopard that day, but there had been others which had performed with equal ferocity, and at times with greater cunning. I thought back to the small female that I had killed in the Himalayas when I had been sixteen years old. It had been the first leopard that I had shot entirely on my own steam and planning, and it had been a maneater as well.

February, 1943 had been dark and dreary, like the snow clouds which hung over the lower Himalayas where my family had come to hide from the war in Burma. My father had been back, briefly, after having been " missing in action " for many months, and now he was out there again on the Assam-Burma front. I had been old enough to shoot a gun very well, I thought, and felt a boy's eagerness to be out with the men to push back the Japanese invaders which had destroyed our home in Burma. I was separated from my favourite hunting companions, the Lahu of Burma and Thailand, and there I was, freezing in an environment very different from the steamy jungles that I had known. The snow lay white on all the rugged hillsides and there were no palms, rattan, nor towering bamboo. But it was a wonderfully different new country to me: of ice and snow, moss and lichen, coniferous forests, and of great mountains which would have awed the Lahu mountain people themselves. Strange game abounded: ghorral, bhurral, tahr, ibex, musk deer, the fabulous snow leopard, screaming monal pheasants, and the wild-cackling koklas, in addition to the many animals that we had in Burma.

The people had been very different from the Lahus that I had grown up with. The " Pahari wallas " of that section of the Himalayas were from various mountain Indian tribes. There were Gharwalis, Kumounis, and many with mixtures of Bhutia or people coming from nearby Tibet. Never had I seen such mountain people. They were a fantastic people, adapted to the incredible struggle for existence in the world's most rugged mountains. A daily routine was to travel, very commonly in bare feet on the snow, thousands of feet up or down those steep hillsides, carrying unbelievable burdens. My own feet never got used to the cold, even with good boots and wool socks.

I remembered the spring months, so different from the cold winters; the country would take on a glorious rapture that cannot be described. The majesty of the great mountains, capped with perpetual snow; the magnificent ibex, horns long and back-curving, standing like a statue on a distant pinnacle, all four feet upon a space the size of your palm; the gentle whistle of the wind through the deodars; the soaring lammagar, a feather loose in his great wing making a rattling sound; and far below, the icy and rushing Aglar murmurs its urgent evacuation of melted snow from Gangotri and Jumnotri far to the north east. And I remembered that lone hermit near Jumnotri who had said as he gazed out over the white mountains, " Great is the Creator of all this splendour!" When the war ended, I had left the Himalayas with reluctance.

Tara Singh, sometime *dudh-walla* and coolie, and certainly one of the best hunting guides in all Mussoorie-pahar, preferred to jaunt with me through the hills for the pittance of four annas per day when such work meant *shikar*. Small of bone, and slight, this intrepid young Gharwali could carry 150-pounds of venison for hours up the brutal climbs. We became more than Sahib and Coolie. Wherever he might be today, he remains the best friend I found in all of India. But the form of Hindi-cum-Urdu which he taught me to speak was of such atrocious idiom that there were times when I was badly embarrassed when trying to use the vernacular with some of India's more affluent society. I decided to abandon any claim to the lovely language when a fine Parsee gentleman in Bombay said of my *pahari-ki-boli*, " My God, man! What happened? Your speech is haw-ri-bahl! How could you . . . how could you . . . how could . . .!"

I had heard of the leopard that had been troubling the several hamlets below Jebharkhet, but it was operating well out of the areas that Tara and I frequented for ghorral and barking deer. We were not interested in wasting nights on the small chance that we might be in the right place at the right time for a particular leopard. But things changed when we began to hear of several deaths reported by *dudh-wallas* who came in to sell milk.

One morning Tara came striding up the hill to the bungalow where we stayed and began talking excitedly about a leopard which had killed a cow belonging to his dear friend, " who is also an unlovely, hateful *bunya-walla.*" I grabbed my shotgun, a 12-gauge " T. Wild " which had belonged to a retired English colonel, and scampered away down the shale landslide with my ragged companion. We half ran all the way, " riding " down landslides for shortcuts whenever possible and arrived at the *bunya* in about an hour. There we were greeted by a sad, pot-bellied man, Tara's " dear friend " and told of the calamity. The man's only milking cow was now gone. Woe was he and his family, and think of the *chota but-chas,* sahib, the little ones would have no milk now. I was certain that the *bunya-walla* would manage somehow, and saw that Tara was enjoying himself immensely watching the man who sold him only five *beedis* instead of six for the price of one hard-earned pice.

The main road from Tehri Gharwal led out from the east end of Mussoorie along one side of the long ridgeline. At several places, hamlets of four or five houses perched precariously at the side of the road overlooking the sheer cliffs. This had been just such a house, half-hung over the brink with a thousand feet between the outer edge of the building and the rocks below. The cow had been taken from the pen under the house, killed quickly, and pushed over the brink to fall far below and away from any further interference from the owner. The leopard might have been discouraged while dragging it down the road, had it used this more usual method. Instead, the killer had used careful plans, striking swiftly and clearing the kill from the scene by the most expedient method. " You see, sahib, it was no ordinary *lakarbhagara,* it had the cunning of *shaitan* (Satan)!" The leopard had used extraordinary tactics, going around later at leisure by a more convenient route to pick up the kill which had tumbled to the bottom of the cliff.

The best trail down was from the right, about five hundred yards up the road. I saw the tracks of a small leopard, fresh in the light dust and thought that the killer could not be this same animal. I had made up my mind that it had to be a large male to handle a full-grown cow in the way it had. But this had been the killer, and it had used this same trail when it went to look for the cow's carcass. We found the cow about a hundred yards from where it had landed, dragged to a small ditch and placed under thickets to keep it safe from crows and vultures. Very little had been eaten from one place on the rump, and it had been successfully kept out of sight from the birds.

Tara and I made a very simple *machan* in a nearby tree, and because it appeared that the leopard might be hiding-out close to the spot, I climbed quickly into my perch and told the Indians to return back to the bunya, making plenty of noise to let the leopard think that we had all gone. There were times later when this trick worked very well, bringing the lurking leopard out almost at once. But it did not work out on that occasion. My leopard had chosen to bed far away and my waiting began from three o'clock in the afternoon until dusk without seeing it return.

Just at dusk a number of different leopards began their coughing calls from various areas to my left and right, down the mountain slopes. A flock of kalij pheasant came scratching up the ridge just behind the dead cow, and I watched them as well as several magpies which had found the carcass and were pecking away at the exposed meat on the rump. Then the kalij began screeching in alarm, increasing their " chee-tik-tik-tik " until they finally took flight. One of them, a hen, came right into my tree. She cocked her head nervously about, craned it forward and took a good look at me before flying away screaming even louder.

Then it was all quiet again. Even the magpies had stopped their noisy calling, and a dark shadow came suddenly around some bushes in front of me. I was about to shoot my first leopard and the thrill of it was almost too much for me. I thought that I was looking at an animal five times its actual size. What had come seemed to be a huge, black tiger, standing there across the shallow ditch, looking right at me. I was shaking uncontrollably, sure that the leaves were dancing up and down along with my trembling and giving away my position.

My "tiger" continued to stand there, looking right at me instead of the cow. Then with a few jerky twitches of its tail, it let out a series of deep-throated growls which became coughs, coming from a lowered head. It had not seen me after all! I felt that I had the element of surprise and became more confident. Had the big cat seen or recognised me, it would not be going through this bit of vocal demonstration. But when would it move into my line of sight? I dared not move the shotgun an inch for fear that the movement would give me away. I was held, cramped tensely, for what seemed a very long time, but actually it must have been only a few minutes.

Without a sound, the leopard leaped easily across the ditch and reached the cow with a few deliberate steps. Suddenly it was a much smaller animal and I was almost disappointed as I took careful aim at the base of the neck and shot. It was the easiest thing in the world to kill a leopard. My first one rolled over quietly and stretched out quivering just beside the dead cow. I did not feel like the *bahut bara shikari sahib* as I cupped my hands around my mouth and hollered for Tara. Surely I had gotten the wrong leopard, a small one at that.

Tara and several Indians came shouting and singing down the ridge, carrying pitch-pine torches. They went immediately up to the leopard, looked at the feet, then started shouting for joy. It *was* the *jebharkhet-ki-shaitani-*

walla they exclaimed, and I was a *bara shikari-walla* for having killed it! The hind foot—they'd know it anywhere —had two claws on the right foot damaged so that they stuck out with claws extended, not returning to the normal retracted position. And besides, the killer they had heard about was supposed to be small, Later, the question that it might be the same one as that which had killed several people became well enough confirmed to satisfy me. My great " male " leopard turned out to be a small female, teeth badly worn, and wounded by several other hunters. The cause for her killing both humans and domestic livestock might have started originally with a porcupine quill which had lodged in the muscles of her neck. She had been famous for her planned attacks, striking at unexpected times and places. We learned that she had operated as far away as Rikkikhesh, twenty-five miles down the valley. After her death we did not hear of any other attacks for as long as I remained in Mussoorie. It was difficult to ascertain her actual crimes, but taken as best we could gather from our later investigations, it appeared that this leopardess had killed four human beings, some fifty goats and sheep, and twenty-two head of cattle in two years.

Thirteen years later, as I sat on a rock in the Mae Suet, thoughts of that first leopard came to me for a very good reason: the sounds which came from the rocky ridge above were so much the same that I could see the other female, head lowered, tail twitching as she called. But the circumstances were very different. She might or might not have located the male's organs which I had tossed up the bank. I heard her growl deeply as she got my scent and realised that the whole thing was a deception. My decoy squeals did not fool her, and with a hoarse cough she moved away up the ridge, never coming out of the scrubby bushes. On the way back to camp, a big porcupine started from behind a rock, grunting loudly like a pig and giving me a start.

I shot him because he was much better eating than a tough old male leopard. In a few minutes, Big Pig and Gems came along to shoulder the burden between a pole. They were delighted.

In camp that night, after the skin had been completely dressed, I leaned back contentedly against a sack of rice to listen to Big Pig's tales of leopards which he had hunted. There was the killer of Ah Maw, a deaf mute hunter, which had almost become "the last walk" for Big Pig himself. The claw marks he showed us on his chest and thighs were part of his thrilling story. Another had taken his freshly killed barking deer and dragged it away while he stood nearby reloading his muzzle-loader. He had followed it and received an attack from behind, but had been so swift with his long knife that the leopard was dead before it touched him.

I had heard these tales before, but never tired of listening to them again, and rolled my hip around to settle it into a little depression. My sudden yell stopped Big Pig in the middle of his story. A wood scorpion had found my settling hip most objectionable, and had sent his stinger solidly into my rear. Gems lifted a leaf, found the specked terror and crushed it, laughing delightedly. "That's too bad, Jaw Maw, these ornery creatures have no respect for Lahus either!" I tried to laugh with them, but I had lost desire to enter the yarn-spinning after that, and tried to take my mind off the tingling burn by walking around the camp. I heard the female leopard calling from far up the ridge, then another leopard and yet another called from the opposite side of the valley. It was the mating season for leopard in the Mae Suet. There was more than one male and female in the area and I felt pleased that I had not robbed an only mate for the leopardess. We would return in April and May to try to find some cubs. And that we did, bringing home "Lena," another most unforgettable leopard in my life.

Despite the usual great danger that a cub is exposed to when snatched from its jungle environment and raised near domestic cats, we were fortunate in bringing up Lena without having her fall victim to feline enteritis. Domestic animals are apparently quite immune, but the cubs of big cats stand in fearful danger of contracting the virus at a critically young age. From a fuzzy little kitten, my wife Peggy bottle-fed her until she developed rapidly to the size when she could eat solids by herself. That had been achieved at considerable and faithful hard work on Peggy's part as she braved the many scratches that Lena inflicted on her hands and wrists while holding the eagerly struggling baby each time the bottle came. Lena would fight like a starved creature, missing the nipple and refusing to settle down until the warm milk began to flow soothingly down her throat. Then she would roll over on her back and sometimes hold the bottle by herself until it was drained, or become furious when it slipped from her paws.

At five months, Lena looked much more mature than she actually was. She was an armful by then, and big enough to bat Sunny, our little cocker spaniel, across the room if she tried to contest a bone. Sphinx-like, she would sit on top of the piano and look at arriving guests unblinkingly. A few thought at first that she might have been a stuffed animal, getting a good jolt when Lena shifted her head. Then there was the mortifying time when the landlady came by to show our four young daughters a sweet little puppy. Without checking first to see where Lena was, the puppy was placed on the floor while everyone admired it. Lena actually loved dogs that she knew, but these were all grown animals that were a good match for her in her daily tussles around the yard. But this tiny creature was different, and it stirred Lena's untried instincts. The catastrophe happened. Lena was off from her sphinx position, sailing through the air, and in one swift—and merciful we hope—motion the little dog was beyond help. Surely we had never faced eviction with more justified reason. But the landlady, a truly great lady, brushed away her tears and forgave us, even the snarling, unrepentant Lena.

Lena was a lovable, incorrigible rascal that we managed to keep out of any further serious misdemeanours. True, she found certain destructive habits much to her liking, such as clawing runs and tears—always in a playful manner —in the stockings and socks of well-dressed visitors. A swat on the head with a rolled newspaper had the opposite effect on her it should have had. As if too proud to accept such chastisement, she would renew her attack against the person who dared to treat her like a common animal. Only a period spent in solitary confinement in her cage would bring her around at such a time. Actually, everything that Lena did had the wild zest of a cub training to become a hunter, and basically these forays were purposefully destructive. At times we were all her " prey "; she leaped out at our legs from behind the couch as we walked by, or launched an aerial attack on one of us from as high as she could climb. Our daughters playing in their sand box received a slow, stealthy, creeping attack from Lena. As low on the grass as she could get, head moving up periodically to check how she was doing, Lena moved closer and closer until the final dash and leap brought her playfully up to the little girls. If she got too rough, Lena received a cuff for her pains, but she was learning by instinct, throughout her playing, with no mother leopard to guide her. Because of her small size, these manoeuvres amused us, but it would have been foolish had we kept her beyond the cub stage in view of our small, slower-growing children.

During the time that Lena shared our home, she showed us much about the inner secrets of the ways of her kind. She exemplified the magnificence of the leopard's untamable nature and an independence that we never saw in other pets. She relished being a proud leopard, padding majestically around our home as though it were her private forest. Her boudoir was atop the grape arbor, where she could gaze at the mountains beyond and sleep undisturbed even when it rained. Had her strength and unpredictable nature remained that of a cub, we would have kept her always. But Lena grew—much too fast. When we had to let her go to a new home in a zoo, we felt an emptiness in the house. Fortunately, she was soon followed by a pair of wonderful Clouded Leopard cubs, and these helped to take our minds away from a great loss. She would always remain as one of our most unforgettable animal friends.

At one time or another since I was a boy of eleven, I met leopards, perhaps a hundred or more. They all had one thing in common—magnificence. Every case that I can recall remains unforgettable, from the cubs that I kept to the man-eaters that I joined other hunters to find. The encounters in the jungles showed me things that set leopards apart from all other wild animals; they are surely the greatest hunters and, when wounded, the most dangerous creature to face.

One hundred and seventy pounds of cat is plenty cat. The largest male leopards that reach this weight and size are completely lethal to man in hand-to-claw combat. It takes a very good man, and few of them live, who could stand up to much smaller leopards with bare hands. A seventeen-hundred pound bull, ten times his weight, is fair game. After he has killed one, the leopard might drag him for miles over all kinds of jungle obstructions. Together with five other men, I tried to drag a dead cow which a female leopard had killed, and this had given us great difficulties even for the few yards. The leopardess had dragged the cow for two miles down a dry stream bed.

Compared to a large male tiger, the biggest leopard looks puny, but ounce for ounce in sheer strength and agility, I would give the odds to "Spots." His smaller size and finer co-ordination allow him greater versatility, aided by tremendous speed and unmatched skill in hunting. When, for unfortunate reasons, he turns against man, he is easily the most cunning and dangerous animal in the jungle. In my experience, every leopard had a special characteristic that I shall not forget, which I cannot say about the tigers that I have met. This is, perhaps, unfair to the greatness of tigers for which I have the highest admiration, but I must give " Spots " the due credit for having at least crossed my trail more consistently with magnificence than any other big cats.

CHAPTER FIVE

Valley of the Bear

" Neh da k'o ya chaw ta meu . . . Ya da k'o yeh chaw ta meu."
" A wise maid leaves boys alone; a wise man leaves bears alone."

THE Mae Tha-lope trail comes to a divide just where the stream itself forks into the mountains. Few travellers take the right fork, which is steep, uninviting and hardly recognisable as a trail that men might use. Mountain people living far above the fork sometimes use the trail to come to favourite fishing spots along the stream. The main trail to the left leads over a high pass before winding around the side of a long mountain range and dropping into Mae Shwe, three days' walk away.

There are a number of old signs indicating that people have camped at the fork on occasions. A discarded bamboo water pipe leaning against a tree could only have been left behind by the Haw, or Yunnanese opium smugglers. It had been careless of them to leave this evidence, but judging from the numerous camp fires, they had been a large gang and probably felt strong enough to be unconcerned at the possibility of running into a police patrol. These were desperate men who felt that dead strangers who had seen them contributed more to their cause than those that walked off. Their motto was simple: *when in doubt, shoot first!*

It was a delightful place to rest. The water was cold and sweet, and a cooling breeze came up the stream. I sat on a rock talking to Ca Meh (Gets Lost), a new man who had joined me for the first time. He knew this section well, and because he had at one time been a carrier on opium gangs, he did not share my anxieties for meeting smugglers in the jungles. " You must not worry, Jaw Maw. I know what to say if we meet them. But just in case they might misunderstand, remember to carry your rifle in your hand or slung with the muzzle forward. Then they will think that we know the customs and not mistake us for government men!" I appreciated the advice, but wished that I had not dressed in old army fatigues which made me look something like a " government man."

My thoughts were still on Haw smugglers when a group of men came around a bend of the trail above us. I jumped up, thinking at first that they might be part of an opium gang, then realised that they were Lahus struggling down the steep trail with difficulty, carrying an awkward burden. As they drew nearer I saw that they had a man on a makeshift bamboo stretcher. When they saw us, they began to jabber excitedly in the colloquial of the Red Lahu. The stretcher was lowered onto a flat rock, just across the stream from where I sat, and the man upon it began to moan.

Pa Suh (New Frog) spoke first, greeting them in Red Lahu which was his own tribe, " What happened, Cousins? What ails your man? "

Several voices chimed in at the same time, " Bear got our brother!" Then one of the older men stepped across the stream and hunkered down near us. He introduced himself as the chief of the Whey Mi (Bear Valley) village. I had never met any of the Lahu from this particular clan before, but they had apparently heard of me through other hill people. He turned to me and said " Jaw Maw, please put medicines on my brother and make him well as quickly as possible! "

I jumped across to the man on the stretcher and could not control my shock. A few weeks before I had come upon a bad bus wreck on the Fang road, and had surprised myself at being able to help with horribly mutilated living and dead human beings without showing much emotion. But this was almost more than I could stand. The stench from gangrene which had set in was unbearable and made me turn, sure that I would vomit. The sight was even worse —much worse than if the man had just been mauled. Filthy bandages made from shreds of old cloth and leaves tied in place with strips of bark, and evil looking concoctions of crushed herbs made into a plaster, covered the torso and most of the man's head. Over the whole sodden mess hovered hundreds of flies, drawn by the stench and going after the wounded man as though he had been dead for days. I walked away a few paces and sat down to get over my initial horror and nausea.

The chief came over to me and squatted down. He smiled, very confident that "The Great White Witch-doctor" could soon summon up many benevolent spirits to take care of the situation. I looked at him sadly and asked him how quickly he and his men could carry the patient to the Fang road. Going hard, they could do this in about seven hours. Then I told him to go directly to the Border Police station and ask them to help in getting transportation to Chiengmai. I scratched out a note to my good friend, Dr. Rubiat, Chief Surgeon at the Government Hospital: "Dear Doc . . . If by some miracle this man arrives alive, know that I am praying for you! Good luck and see you next week. Gordon."

I was quite overcome with pity for the wounded man and for the simple faith that these people had in the "white man's medicine." I was supposed to be a doctor and a worker of miracles as far as they were concerned. I had, with sulfa drugs and penicillin, helped a few people from the Pumuen clan across the valley, and the reports that had come to them had become exaggerated in the process so that they bordered on the impossible. I spoke to the chief in language that he could best understand.

" Chief, it happens sometimes that the wrath of the spirits is so strong that it takes many medicine men in a big house to overcome such as has happened to your man. So everything depends upon whether or not this man is still living by the time he reaches Chiengmai. Meanwhile, I will try to give him ' strength' medicines to help along the way. This is a job for a much bigger medicine man!" He nodded understanding and placed my note to Dr. Rubiat in his bag while I opened my rucksack.

I had a small medic's kit with me which very fortunately had sulfa powder, penicillin and battle dressings that army friends had given me. I had anticipated serious wounds if any one of us ever did get mixed up with dangerous game, and had also replenished my kit after the bus-wreck experience. But I had nothing left when I got through with the first aid on the Lahu man. I could only hope that in the next week, we would not be faced again with another badly wounded man. It was something like starting off on a long car trip on bald tyres, without a spare, or tools to fix a flat.

The unbelievable mess that I started in on had even appalled my doctor friends later. It was one of the most difficult undertakings that I have ever forced myself to do. First, after removing the filthy rags, I had two men stand nearby swatting away the flies. Often, these would be smashed right into the opened wounds. The right eye had been forced out of its orbit and hung shrivelled against the cheek. I nipped this away with my scissors. Both cheeks had been fractured and lacerations covered the face from the bear's jaws. The claws had done much more, having removed whole slabs of skin from the torso, mostly on the left shoulder. Gangrene had set in throughout this area, and I felt that the man would probably lose his left arm. I started out with a massive dose of penicillin, then tried my best to clean up the wounds with soap and water. I dusted all the wounds with sulfa powder and used all my

96

bandages to cover them. When I got through with him, he looked neater anyway, but I felt as though I had played the part of a mortician rather than a medic. The man appeared to be too far gone. I gave him a chance in a thousand to reach Chiengmai. But he did reach Chiengmai alive, and " Doc " Rubiat performed some of the finest surgery and plastic surgery work possible to save the man. We still call it a miracle.

When the Lahus had gone, we continued on up the trail from which they had come and reached their village at dusk. My original plans had been to go through this area to Mae Shwe, stopping at various hill villages to trap and shoot leopards. I had come with three Lahu boys instead of the usual gang which accompanied me on treks away from villages. The bear mauling changed my plans. When the villagers had told me the story and urged me to try to kill the bear for them, I decided to give it a try. It was an excellent way in which to get to know the Whey Mi Lahus. If I was successful in getting the bear, I could depend on them to help me later on in the business of collecting natural history specimens in their area.

No one had followed the bear after finding the mauled man six days before. It had been a big male which roamed the area between Whey Mi and several other Lahu villages nearby. It had mauled nine people, killing all but three of them, including the man we had just seen. The bear had been aggressive only when met in the jungles; it had never sought the people out deliberately, as I learned when the facts were finally sorted out from numerous additions to each maul case. It had been wounded a number of times, both by bows and by muzzle-loading guns. The last victim had been hunting silver pheasant when the bear suddenly reared up from behind a log. The man had promptly released the arrow into the bear's chest and tried to flee. He was caught when he got hung up in rattans, and the bear had not spared him a terrible punishment. He should have

97

forgotten about the useless bird arrow and moved away carefully.

The next morning I took New Frog and Gets Lost with me to a field where the bear's tracks had been seen the day before. It did not take us long to find the fresh tracks among the pumpkins down at the edge of the last of two fields near the stream. There could be no mistaking this one! The villagers had said, " Just follow the biggest tracks, that's the one. We know only of this one really big bear around here." I was looking at the biggest tracks of a Himalayan bear that I had ever seen, with front pugs eight inches wide. These tracks were an inch wider and longer than anything that I had called big before. I started out in great spirits, happy that we had the whole day ahead in which to track. It seemed unlikely that we would need to follow him very far—he was too big and too bold to be worried about getting far away from dangers that for him did not exist. I felt that he would bed down within a few hundred yards of the pumpkin field so that he would have easy, leisure access to it again on the following night.

As we took the tracks up the other side of the small stream, I thought about the various precautions that I needed to take. The Tibetan or Himalayan bear (Selenarctos tibetanus) is the " grizzly " of Southeast Asia, or certainly its equivalent in temperament. It is agile both on the ground and in trees, and because of its cunning men have run into trouble with them. They are tough brutes to kill or turn in a charge, sometimes rolling down a hillside and presenting a difficult target. An experienced killer used such tricks as reversing its direction after turning in a " U " to take up ambush positions to one side of its original track. While their sense of smell is very acute, I have learned that their hearing and eyesight is very respectable as well, contrary to some popular beliefs. I had every intention to be at my cautious best that day.

The tracking was easy at first because the ground was soft

under the thick trees, but after the bear passed this shaded area, his tracks were mere scuffs on hard, dry earth. He had the annoying habit of taking logs, or jumping from rock to rock to leave very little sign. Soon I realised that he was out for a good long walk before settling down for a nap. We had started out at 6.30 that morning and it was noon before we realised it. The bear had taken various ridges and stayed out of ravines which were his logical bedding areas. It seemed that he was moving directly away from the fields, but we learned later that he had been skirting in a wide circle and moved back towards the fields from the left. So far he had moved deliberately, with a general course in mind, not stopping for any of the usual distractions that bear are prone to investigate. I stopped with the two Lahu men on a small ridge and we ate our lunch of cold rice and salted meat.

About mid-afternoon we followed the tracks along the side of a steep hillside well-shaded by tall *mai sang* bamboos. At one place, an entire clump of bamboo had fallen over a small bank, presenting a solid barrier. The bear had chosen to go under the fallen bamboos instead of circling them, and I decided to do the same to save a little time. The space was just enough to crawl through without much difficulty; the bear was nowhere in sight, and I was not concerned that he might suddenly rush out while I was in that awkward position inside the bamboos. Another, possibly much surer, form of death awaited me just there. With my face low to the ground, left hand supporting me and my rifle in my right hand, I froze. A small cobra, its head raised and small hood spread, quivered not more than five inches from my nose. Had I been looking down the barrel of a loaded bazooka, I could not have been more terrified. The potent little serpent, some two feet in length, a species from the mountains with which I was not familiar, stared at me, daring me to so much as bat an eye. I held my breath and inched back while the cobra swayed slightly and seemed to vibrate, yet it did not hiss as do larger cobras in their aposematic behaviour. I knew enough about the nature of cobras to realise that even if this was a young snake, its venom would be fatal, especially when introduced into so sensitive an area as the nose. It was not only the most awkward situation I have ever stumbled into, it was as close to death as I have been in my life!

As I inched backwards, I brought the muzzle of my rifle up so that it soon interposed between my face and the snake. Then I struck out with the muzzle and shoved the reptile to one side, following up quickly by beating it against the ground. When I had killed it, dirt had filled the end of the barrel and had to be removed before we continued our tracking. My two companions thought the incident was very funny. I could not share their humour as I sat for a few moments smoking nervously after cleaning my rifle. That brief encounter will always remain huge in my memories. As the Lahus say, " The jungle has many lessons —you may see a speck or you may see a mountain, but look for the specks as well as the mountains! "

By 3.00 p.m. we did not seem to be getting any nearer to the bear, which had been travelling without any apparent purpose, moving in and out of unlikely places as far as good bedding spots went. My patience was beginning to run out, and I found that I was not always observing good caution. It would soon be necessary to leave the tracking in order to allow enough daylight to find our way back to the village. I decided to give it one more hour.

After moving along a small ridge between two shallow ravines, the bear's tracks led to the right side and passed a landslide just above its head. He had, for some reason, reached the far side then doubled back again to stand centred above the landslide. His tracks seemed to vanish there and we spent several minutes trying to find out where he had gone. It turned out to be a remarkable trick of hiding tracks. The bear had leapt straight down the landslide, clearing it without leaving any marks, to land on a large protruding rock twenty feet below. From the rock he had jumped again, clearing the low bushes and landing beside the trickle of water in the stream. The jolt from these leaps might have loosened the bear's bowels, because he had left a great pile of partially-digested pumpkins near the place he had landed.

Now the tracking became ghastly for about fifty yards. The ravine was matted with rattans in that section which clawed and pulled at my body with every step. The bear had taken wild pig trails under the rattan and we followed at a very low stoop. I knew that the bear had been as anxious as we were ourselves to get through the rattan, and that there was small chance that he would have chosen a place in those thorns to bed down. There are few living creatures that can move about easily in rattans, and bears especially have a strong aversion to them. We struggled on through, not worrying about the noise we made just there.

As though relieved that he had finally broken out from an inadvertent misdirection into rattan, the bear had paused just beyond this matted stand to pull down several stalks of wild bananas and chew out the juicy hearts. Then he had rolled about in the damp weeds, ridding himself of the dried, brittle thorns which had clung to his fur. The side of a small sapling was still damp where he had rubbed before moving down the ravine.

I had been so busy tracking the bear that it was some time before I realised that we had come into *mai mo* bamboos. I became aware of this when I suddenly noticed that it had become very gloomy and dark under the shadows of the low-hanging bamboos. It was just going on 4.00 p.m. and yet it seemed like dusk had closed in on us. Slowly the truth dawned on me: we were right in the middle of a bear's favourite bedding area.

Mai mo is a type of trailing bamboo which clings low to the ground in heavily matted piles. Underneath these canopies are tunnels which weave in and around the different clumps of each stand of bamboos. In very old stands such as this one, the tunnels are tightly closed in, but well defined from the movements of pig, sambar deer and bear. A man can either stoop low through them or crawl, and he is recognised as a fool for doing so when such a place harbours a bad-tempered bear. A favourite saying in Lahu litigations came to mind: "The man who sues without good evidence is like the man crawling around in the *mai mo!*" I should have been in a different "court room" where my opponent could not make such a successful counterclaim. Visibility was limited to some ten yards when peering down through the tunnels, but around every bamboo clump, even a few feet away, the bear might have hidden out of sight to me. I was certainly in his favourite "court room" and New Frog, who had my shotgun as a supporting gun, was of no mind to contest a bear here. I soon realised that I was being politely allowed to proceed by myself carrying my ·30/o6 Springfield. My better judgement screamed in my ears to give it up.

I was no longer looking for tracks, devoting all of my attention in search of a big, black object hidden somewhere in front, to the right, or to the left of me. The humidity seemed to be at saturation point and gnats hovered around, trying to get into my eyes and ears. I checked and rechecked my rifle, making sure it was ready to shoot. Moving at a squat, I was doing about one yard a minute, slow enough that I made no noise, avoiding meticulously every sprig of bamboo which might spring as I brushed it. What I might expect should be plenty of warning, I thought. The bear would snort loudly, clack noisily for a few minutes before rushing out. And he was a big target, even slow on the start. There was no reason for my excitement, I told myself. I was doing so well that I would probably find the bear before he saw me, raising a sleep-drugged head and waiting lazily for my unhurried shot.

A small tree shrew scrambled about in the bamboos to my right, springing twigs of dead wood and causing me to whirl around to face the sound. It was a humbling experience. I was too tense, and in this condition capable of making a mistake. All shooters have taken a quick shot at some time or another to discover that they had a dud round or an empty chamber. To the shooter, *that* was not the important thing. The truth that he might have discovered was that he *flinched* when he squeezed the trigger. I had done the equivalent of a flinch when the little shrew unnerved me. And so, like the shooter who resolves not to flinch on the next shot, I told myself to be calm and steady. I thanked the little shrew for the reminder.

Ten minutes later, and without having progressed more than five or six short steps, I looked at a well-rubbed place in the damp hollow of an old wild boar's nest. The bear had bedded here and left the spot so recently that a musky, wet-dog smell still lingered. I slipped one knee to the ground and waited, watching every dark shadow around the bamboos in a silence that might have been in the depths of some deep cave. The bear had been warned of my approach even though I had been very quiet. He had moved out minutes before I reached the spot, but why had I not seen him? The flicker of a small bird and the tree shrew had drawn my attention immediately, but this huge brute had shifted position like a noiseless phantom. Later, I realised what had happened: *I had moved too slowly*. The air, barely moving towards the bear, had carried my scent to warn him. Had I moved slightly faster, I might have surprised him by keeping abreast of the air which carried my scent. But his silent reactions to my approach were disconcerting—he was behaving in a mysterious manner, unlike an ordinary wild creature adversary. At other times I had come right up to a napping bear, surprising it even though I had come downwind because I had been moving fast. All bears that I had met before had raised their voices, usually with the typical clacking sounds when they discovered my presence or scent. I should not have thought that all the people who had been mauled by this bear had been careless, nor should I have underestimated his potential cunning. He had planned a nice little ambush for me and it was now an even game of hunter versus hunter. I had a good rifle with probably only one shot to go—he had his choice of battle grounds and very close quarters.

Bamboos are the undoing of many a good hunter as well as the game. Many times my bullets had deflected off the tough stalks and sprigs, missing the mark completely or registering a poor hit. Hidden stalks had tripped me, once to sprain my ankle very badly, and at other times to warn the big game by the twanging, rattling noise. For some, it had meant much more serious misadventure. For all hunters who have been in bamboos, a certain twig has earned his curses at some place or another. My bear on this occasion was first to get into trouble with bamboo. It was a very small thing, but enough to force him to move before he had intended, thus spoiling his well-laid ambush. For once I blessed all bamboos, even *mai mo*.

The sound had been much more subtle than that made by the tree shrew. When the bear had raised his head to look at me from a hollow behind a clump of bamboo, he had sprung a small sprig. A small wren might have produced the same faint sound. I focused all my attention in the direction where I had heard the sound, just to my left. The bear was looking right at me now from the dark shadows into which he blended perfectly, no more than ten yards away. The shadow was an oblong mass which suddenly changed its shape as the bear rolled out towards me and became discernible for the first time. I was not hearing any sounds at all as I sought out the bear's head low to the ground. The lighter colour of the muzzle gave me a clue to a good head shot, and I let the round go just above the bear's snout when he had surged forwards to within five yards of me. The roar of my Springfield in that closed-in ravine was very reassuring and the bear dipped his head to the ground and rolled over to one side on his back. It " did not speak before it died," as New Soul said later. My 220-grain bullet had gone neatly through the nasal cavity and shattered the base of the skull. I fired at the quivering form once again for good measure and broke the neck three inches below the skull. Then I sat down squarely on the ground, and felt a great weight of tension lift from me. I was suddenly very elated.

Lying on his back, with all fours in the air, was the greatest Himalayan bear that I had seen. I wished that I could have weighed and measured him for purposes of his accurate comparison with other big specimens of his species. Another bear had scaled at just over five-hundred pounds and that individual had been considerably smaller. I feel, therefore, that my estimate of around six-hundred pounds for this one may not have been too far off. The skull, which I had taken carefully back to Chiengmai, was stolen from my collection before proper measurements could be recorded.

Clearly visible in the white of the " V " on the bear's chest was a small scab which covered the puncture from the last victim's arrow. As I skinned the animal, I made an incision at the site of the arrow wound and found that it had been a penetration of about one inch. We skinned the animal quickly, bundled up the hide and skull, and moved out from the bamboos, thinking that we had some eight miles or more to do before we reached the village. The field from which we had started out was, instead, only about a mile away. There we found a juicy cucumber melon and sat for a few moments enjoying its cool, refreshing goodness before heading up the hill.

At the top of the ridge we were back on the trail that led to the Lahu village. We relaxed our pace and walked casually along, happy hunters coming back from a day's hard work, not looking for any more excitement. In this carefree manner, with myself walking along in the lead, the three of us walked right into an ambush of some fifty opium smugglers who had heard us coming down the trail. I saw the first man squatting partially concealed behind a tree with an automatic weapon aimed at me. I stopped and almost raised my rifle, but checked myself in time. Others materialised from different positions and the leader shouted something just then. Had I raised my rifle, I might well have been shot on the spot. They saw, just in time, that there were only three of us, and I was carrying my weapon *at a trail in my hand!* I burbled out almost at once, trying to sound very cheerful, "Friends! Don't shoot!"

The Yunnanese leader ordered something I could not understand, then I heard the words, "Pu suh" (negative) and I felt a relief that made me want to shout with joy. They were everywhere, tumbling out from hastily prepared positions above and below the trail, coming back onto the trail. I walked up to them, glad to be alive and yet not feeling at all happy about running into them. My best manners and nonchalance were important now—I still had a chance of being taken along or left headless below the road just because we had met. Nobody was sure of anything up to that point and more guns appeared, most of them still aimed at me and the two Lahus behind me. Gets Lost, who said he knew just what to say, had not come through, still trying to find his voice. I gave the smugglers my finest smile and spoke out in Lahu, "How are you all, *friends?* It is a nice evening for travelling!" I know that I sounded very shaky and self-conscious, but they seemed to like that.

"What are you doing along this trail?" the leader said in the more polite form of Lahu speech. I relaxed when

I heard the good command of Lahu, the faintly recognisable friendliness, and found my own voice again.

"Coming from the hunt—we got the big bear that's been killing folks around here," I replied, trying very hard to get them all interested at once in this fact. I never felt more reassured when to my surprise many of the smugglers started cheering. The American Consul at Chiengmai might not need to take the long hike into the hills after all to investigate the strange disappearance of a taxpayer!

I sat down, inviting the leader and several men in the front of the column to do the same, and thought how to get them to stop the annoying habit of pointing loaded guns at me. At this point I decided against an over-friendly, humble approach. The tricky phase of initial contact was over when misunderstandings could have led to a number of guns going off. So I said, almost angrily, "Tell your men to take their guns off me! A man meets friends in the hills and has to be treated like an enemy?"

The Chinaman looked shocked and showed embarrassment. He turned on his men with a terrible face, "You stupid animals! Put down your guns!" Then he cursed in the colourful adjectives for which Yunnanese muleteers are famed and turned to apologise most eloquently. I flicked my hand in a casual gesture and told him that the whole thing was quite understandable. He should not shoot me, I should not shoot him. After all, hadn't we all been on the same side? I knew that he had been a former member of the Chinese *Kou-ming-tang* and referred to the fact that we had mutual enemies within the Mao Tze Tung set.

"There are many of you and only three of us with two guns between us. If you people come as guests, they're too many of you; if you come to fight they're not enough of you!" I laughed to emphasise my joke and all of the smugglers who heard roared with laughter. "Now that we know each other," I said (although we really did not), " we ought to chat awhile before going our ways."

" Yes, yes, yes," my fine brigand exclaimed, " it is good to sit down awhile and talk."

I took the opportunity to introduce myself and to satisfy the man's suspicions that I might have come for the purpose of spying out the activities of opium smugglers. It appeared that he had heard of me through various Lahus that he had met, and the conversation turned to good hunting areas and the bear that we had just killed. Until then I was technically still under arrest, but by the time we had talked about the war in Burma, the Japanese, his former KMT 93rd division and even General " Vinegar Joe " Stillwell, I felt that we could part without sounding off the guns. In fact, my " friend " became almost too sociable, offering me cough drop after cough drop which he produced from a small tin that he carried in his breast pocket. I learned that charming social custom from him and made it a point to carry some myself for the same purpose.

He was a powerfully built Chinaman from the southernmost part of Yunnan. When he smiled, a solid row of gold gleamed from his upper front teeth. He wore the faded blue uniform of the KMT guerillas, worn canvas shoes and a waterproof cap made of plastic material. In addition to the heavy Bren-gun he carried, a Browning automatic pistol protruded from a green money belt at his waist. A hand grenade was tucked away just behind the wire buckle of the belt, and incongruously alongside this was a tube of Colgate's toothpaste. The toothbrush he carried in his breast pocket and he took this out each time he reached for another cough drop. He was extremely generous with the cough drops, insisting that I needed another one as soon as one dissolved in my mouth. " Very good for long walks in the mountains," he explained.

There were many strange faces studying me curiously behind the Chinaman. They were a motley lot, dressed in several different types of shirts and trousers that identified some as Lisu, Akha, Lahu and Meo tribesmen. At least every fifth man carried some sort of automatic weapon: old U.S. Army " grease-guns," a Browning automatic rifle, Thomson submachineguns, British Stenguns and the Bren-gun that the leader carried. These had been obtained from dubious sources after the Japanese conflict in Burma. I realised that most of the carriers were tribesmen, recruited specially for the job, and the automatic weapons were carried by the Yunnanese escorts. The packs containing the raw opium were made up in tight bundles which were strapped on the men's backs with *pakamas* or waist cloths. Not all of the men carried arms, but enough non-Chinese were carrying some sort of weapon that they must have been regular carriers who could be trusted. This gang did not lack fire-power. They might have needed it, because they were packing about one ton of opium.

As a man, I could not dislike this sturdy traveller. His was a despicable trade, governed by many unfortunate circumstances, and for which he represented only a very small cog in a big piece of machinery. He had a hand, sometimes directly, in the ruination and even death of innocent people. He might have shot me and my two companions and laughed about it. The jungle, which is impartial, allowed him and his cohorts to try their hand at a precarious prosperity. His brother, who might have been the man selling noodles on a street corner, was much more to be admired in the light of human morals. I might have understood if it had been the jungles which called this man to a life of adventure in the mountains.

The sun had disappeared over the high ridges to the west when I stood up and announced that we would have to be getting along. As a sort of guarantee that there might not be a shot or two to send us along after our backs were turned, I released a stinker of a joke which I knew would suit their tastes. It went over with resounding success and, amid a clattering of weapons, the smugglers lined up as though they were starting off in the early hours of morning. I watched them file off down the trail into the dusk. The leader was quite genuine, I believe, when he expressed regrets that he could not tarry longer, and wished he had more opportunity to chat about the world beyond the bamboo trails. " We have work to do, you understand? " he had said. It was a type of work that necessitated marching off into the night and not always being polite to strangers met along the trail.

When we had gotten well along the trail, I turned to Gets Lost, " Next time I want you to speak up faster! I thought you were supposed to be good at dealing with these people, you old bandit! "

He gave me a sheepish smile, " Jaw Maw, you said just the right thing and didn't need my help. Besides, you needn't have worried. I would have drawn my knife and come to your rescue! "

I reached over and tousled his unkempt shock of hair and the three of us had a good laugh together. As we continued towards the village he said slowly and thoughtfully, " Come to think of it, there *were* too many of them! "

Just at the head of the village, four little boys sat waiting for us on a large ant hill. When they saw us coming down the trail, they began to jabber excitedly and ran to meet us, peering closely at the bear's head in the near darkness. Then they were gone, bare feet thudding a rapid cadence on the beaten trail, shrill voices heralding the news to the villagers. In a little while the whole village was alive with shouts and a din of barking dogs. We walked proudly into the chief's house and were ourselves very glad.

CHAPTER SIX

Boars from the Rattan

" He va g'aw chu tzuh ve hk'e chaw ya hai chu tzuh ve yo."
" Rattan thorns stick (and anger) the bear;
Gossip thorns stick (and anger) any man."

NEW Frog and I paused on the grassy bluff to scan the small meadow some thirty yards below us. To our right the tall broomgrass began to rustle and a pig grunted several times as it neared the edge of the clearing. We slipped down quietly onto our stomachs to watch from prone positions behind the knee-deep grass.

The old sow poked her head through the broomgrass stalks and glared around her for a few moments through small, suspicious eyes and sniffed the air. Then she gave a series of deep grunts and stepped out into the clearing, showing us what ugliness can amount to in old sows. She was devoid of hair on head and back, crusted with dried mud, and her teats hung loose and wrinkled. She was at least a great, great, great grandmother, and led a good-sized herd behind her. It turned out to be an enormous herd of over sixty wild pigs which came filing out from several different trail openings after she had sounded the " all clear."

There were other great grandmothers, grandmothers, mothers, aunts, a few young uncles and fathers, and more babies than we could count. Soon it was a mass of black and grey which covered the entire clearing below. A number of the sows had yellow-striped babies grouped tightly under their bellies as the herd wandered slowly towards the wet marshes to the left of the meadow. I had never seen wild sows with pigs which returned to the herd while the babies were yet small. But then, the whole activity taking place below me was one which human eyes would seldom witness in the thickets-loving ecology of the Asiatic wild pig. I had chanced, by very lucky coincidence, to be just at the right place at the right time.

The grand old lady of the herd stood motionless just at the edge of the clearing while her huge family continued to fill the clearing from what seemed an endless supply. It was still quite early in the morning, so few of them cared to wallow in the cool marshes. Instead, they began systematically to root and grub in the soft turf, grunting noisily now and giving no heed to the bluff above them. How often, I thought, had a leopard or tiger lain here, waiting for a herd of pigs to become too relaxed, springing down from the bluff to claim a juicy young animal. The old sow could remember, for she kept gazing nervously in our direction, sniffing the air which was actually in our favour. New Frog and I did not move a muscle. A single " Grrrmmp " from her would have sent the whole herd scampering off into the protective covering of the broom-grass.

One of the young boars ventured too close to a sow with pigs and received a vicious bite on the flank. He coughed loudly and ran to one side squealing. Two young females engaged for a time in what looked like two angry ladies in a hair-pulling contest. Ladies can look so ungraceful when they fight. A gilt in the centre of the herd was in heat and a young boar was trying unsuccessfully to mount her. Soon he was expelled from the scene by another young boar which was even smaller in size. The small boar managed the servicing, hanging long over the gilt while the others in the herd continued grubbing about the meadow.

Off to our right, from where the herd had first come,

the broomgrass swayed in a wake which marked the approach of a large animal. This should have been a buffalo or gaur because the movement was much larger than anything the pigs had made. I knew that it could not be a tiger, and the thought made me look behind me up the slope to see if a tiger might have manoeuvred into such a position of vantage. When I turned again to look at the grass, the champion herd boar had come out of the tall stalks and was standing just at the edge of the clearing. I stifled a gasp and felt New Frog pinching me excitedly. The boar was chomping noisily, clacking his tusks in sounds like two fist-sized rocks being knocked together. He strode majestically into the herd, paused to sniff a sow's behind, lost interest, and continued towards the marshy area. The young boars moved respectfully out of his path, and even the grouchy sows with pigs did not protest his presence. He was three times as big as the average sow.

I had no desire whatsoever to shoot this magnificent creature, although New Frog was getting ready to yell his exasperation at me. It was a sight that I shall never forget. He was easily the finest specimen of *Sus scrofa* that it had ever been my pleasure to see. As he stepped out into the morning sun, his coat, clean from a dip in the stream, glowed a reddish-gold sheen. The hair rippled from heavy muscles over the back and flanks as he slashed at a clump of willows, the strips of bark clinging to his tusks. Long, greyish whiskers swept back from the jaws, accentuating the upward curve of the long tusks. He bore his massive weight with an amazing lightness, and seemed to flow along as he walked through the herd. Standing high on the hoof, his back was arched and his body smooth and compact. The long hair along the crest stood thick, sweeping backwards and not yet hoary with age. He was, at least for the time being, the undisputed herd champion. Somewhere, another great boar was living alone, privately training to try some day to take away his office. Then, if he were defeated, he would become a loner himself, unless the boar of another herd could be beaten in terrible battle. But he was still young, in prime condition, fast and accurate, and those tusks were like sabres. I wanted him to stay that way, siring his calibre of offspring. To New Frog those tusks were priceless hunter's charms, and he was definitely unhappy with me just then.

As I watched the big boar disappear slowly into the willows at the far end of the meadow, my mind was still trying to fathom wild pig ecology. Of the many baby pigs scampering near their mothers, only a few of them would live to become adults. Tiger, leopard, wild dogs, and even the golden cat would take a toll of the young pigs before they left their parent's side. Only the larger boars were immune to predatory big cats, and some of these died from battle wounds with other boars. But the wild pig is not a dying race, even where man has taken over his grazing grounds. They are hardy creatures, able to survive in dense second growth jungles which man leaves after slashing and burning the forests for agricultural purposes. The predators tend to disappear quicker from an area than do the pigs, which then increase in number. The lone boars encountered are in two distinct categories: those that are *growing* to maturity and those that have finally been *defeated* as potential herd boars. All boars are potentially dangerous when encountered by man, but this depends entirely upon the particular circumstances. The wounded boar is *always* dangerous for understandable reasons, and so is the herd boar because of his possessive instinct. The loner might charge away and be as shy as any animal to be found in the jungle, especially the younger ones, but there are those individuals that carry a grudge against anything that moves. These are the animals most frequently met by hunters and which give the reputation of fierce temperament to the wild boar. There is a lot to learn about wild pigs in general, especially the herd boar, as I was to learn that morning. I was to become a wiser hunter who never claims to know exactly what to expect in different given situations.

When a sprig of bamboo twanged behind me, I thought at once that a tiger had stalked up, and even hoped that this was the case as I turned my head to look up the slope. New Frog and I were both lying flat, facing away from the sound, and looked back over our left shoulders towards the snapping bamboo. The big boar had worked around from the willows, climbed unnoticed up a gully to the left of our bluff and now stood above and behind us, looking squarely at the two of us. The sight of that great brute with tusks gleaming, no more than fifteen yards away, made us freeze, necks strained in that awkward position. The shock could not have been greater had we found ourselves suddenly looking down the muzzle of a cannon, fuse spluttering and ready to explode any second. In an instant the tables had been turned, and now we were the fine pair of sitting ducks. The boar had only to launch out quickly—there were no obstructions along his line of charge. I had the sickening feeling that at least one of us would be hurt or even killed that morning.

Slowly, because the boar just stood there, realities began welling up in my mind. My rifle lay beside me, muzzle pointing away towards the meadow, and I was leaning on my right elbow which was alongside the rifle. I could not move to bring it into position without a lot of movement, which would surely provoke the boar into immediate charge. If we remained in that position much longer, the boar might finally give us up or he might still charge, depending upon how sure he was of what we were. Then it dawned on me that he was downwind and getting our scent. The boar confirmed my fears by jerking his head up and down a few times, inviting us to so much as bat an eyelash. I was trying to appear motionless while very slowly bringing my right hand into contact with my rifle. I said to myself, "If you can get that gun into position—Oh, dear Lord, may I do so!—then remember to snap the safety off too, and roll like mad out of the way. Don't worry about how scratched up you might get when you fall over the bluff—anything is better than those tusks!"

The boar seemed to be laughing at me, tossing his head up and down again and making jerky challenging motions with his fore hooves. He was now clacking loudly and snorting fearfully. Ten minutes before I had thought that this was the most beautiful pig that I had ever seen; now I was looking with real fear at what seemed the ugliest, most terrifying creature I had faced. With my neck thus craned and getting stiff, I seemed to be losing the perspective to know which direction would be best for clearing away from the charge when it came. I was extremely fortunate in having an experienced Lahu by my side just then who had the nerve not to panic too soon and invite the charge before more preparation, if any, could be made. New Frog and I passed mental notes, unspoken, which said, "It's every man for himself, try to be the one who goes home!"

I had underestimated the big boar before, and now I underestimated him again. Although he had the full advantage just then, he made one little mistake—or was it because he was a gentleman, giving his victims just one little fighting chance? He moved parallel to us a few paces, probably in order to line us up at a lesser angle with the edge of the bluff. In that brief instant I had my rifle in my hands and had swung around to a sitting position. Without a pause in his manoeuvring, the boar let out an ear-splitting cough, almost a blast, and swung right into a charge. I heard New Frog give a yelp as he dived straight out and over the bluff. In long leaps, the boar came down the slope straight at me, whoofing and coughing loudly, not unlike the sounds from a charging leopard. From then on, the only picture I had of the boar as he increased in size through my rifle sights was a blur. I had snapped the safety off through subconscious effort, a reflection of what I had instructed myself to do earlier or I would have died that morning. Sure that I was too late I squeezed the trigger and sprawled off to my right as a spray of dirt and small stones showered me. I continued to scramble along the bluff's edge crazily and knew fright very intimately.

With a tremendous crash the boar landed behind and below me, plunging over the bluff into the thickets. There seemed to be movements everywhere as I worked another round into my rifle. Pigs were rushing in every direction below me, grunting and coughing as they disappeared into cover. The boar thrashed heavily some ten yards below and I heard New Frog scream over to the right. He was well in the clear and it puzzled me to hear him yell frantically continuing his shouts even when I tried to call to him.

I took another shot at the struggling boar and realised that he was not moving from the spot in which he had landed. Then I rushed over to the bluff's edge just over New Frog and tried to determine the cause of his agonies. He had leapt over the bluff, landed some fifteen feet below and scrambled to his right as the boar crashed by him. From there he had gone headlong into heavy wildrose bushes and gotten tangled in the thorns. The cause of his desperate yelling was from another, almost improbable source. Secured solidly by the thorns, my unfortunate companion had dislodged a whole nest of hornets! " Run from the tiger and meet the bear," as he said later. With a final effort of crazy power, New Frog broke out from his thorny bonds and crawled into some thick bushes, still whimpering pathetically, and crying, " Jaw Maw, don't come this way!"

Later we could laugh about it all, but just then neither one of us had reasons to even smile. I was deeply concerned about New Frog, and he was in excruciating agony. Torn from dozens of thorn rips and bruised by rocks, the lad was trying his best to be quiet as a near lethal number of hornets stung him. In addition to this, his confusion had not allowed him to realise that the boar was dead.

"Stay where you are, New Frog," I yelled, "the boar is dead but the hornets still fly about!" I found a place to slide down the bluff to the left of the boar and approached it cautiously. Then I circled well clear of the angry hornets and found New Frog. He could not move and I thought he was slowly fainting away from pain. I put my rifle down and pulled him down the bluff's slope into the clearing, feeling guiltily responsible for getting the fine boy into such a mess. At first glance he seemed much worse than he actually was, but even temporarily, a man could hardly fall into such a miserable state in so short a time. The multiple hornet stings might have killed a lesser man, and I have never seen such a case of thorn lacerations.

I fumbled in my kit bag and the best I could come up with was some aspirin tablets. I gave New Frog four tablets and told him to lie still while I pulled out numerous rose thorns from his arms, face and chest. He smiled faintly and said, "One minute we were made stone by a big boar, then the whole world came tumbling down like a landslide!" He was a sick boy, but I knew that he was not hypersensitive to wasp and hornet stings, and that when the initial burning wore off, he would be up and around again. In any case, it was time to make contact with the other men of our party. I raised my rifle and fired off three rapid shots. From about a mile up the valley, a shot answered my signal. Lighting two cigarettes, I gave one to New Frog and we sat waiting for the other men to join us.

In about twenty minutes a whoop sounded just above us and New Soul came rapidly out of the bamboos, having homed in on my three shots with unerring accuracy.

Shortly after that Big Pig came in from the opposite side of the valley and ran up to us.

"The witches and devils of the hills and dales! What has happened to New Frog?" he exclaimed.

I explained the happenings to Big Pig and he thought that the whole thing was as funny a joke as any he had heard. After a hearty laugh, he assured New Frog that his chances for marrying a beautiful maiden were gone and added, "You look like you had been mauled by seven wildcats!"

Digging into his bag, Big Pig brought out a wad of mountain tobacco and stuffed it into New Soul's mouth. "Chew it well," he said, "and don't spit out the juice so that some of your manhood may yet be preserved!"

With that he laughed again and New Frog amazed me by joining him. A week later, with the scabs still on his face, New Frog married Big Pig's daughter, one of the prettiest girls in the village.

By the time we had butchered the boar and had the meat packed into hastily-made bamboo baskets, New Frog had gotten over the stings and was ready to shoulder a pack himself. We went back up on the bluff to study the scene of the charge. The boar's deep hoof prints showed that he had made leaps of fifteen feet and more as he came down the slope. I sat at the spot where he had originally stood to look at us; it was a clear view, and from that perspective the bluff looked too shallow to be of any concern in case it was overshot. He had probably cleared the distance in two seconds. My bullet had struck the boar just above the left eye when he was about five yards from me, causing him to dip away to that side, and throwing him into a head-over-end somersault as he passed me. New Frog and I both assumed our old positions again and showed the two men what he had done. Talking excitedly as we demonstrated our separate gymnastics, we both worked ourselves into a sweat and came out trembling as we relived that moment.

Far up the mountain's side came a mournful whistling which mounted up into a brisk " Pee-o-peet, pee-o-peet." New Soul looked at me and smiled, " Hear what he is saying? " In Lahu, the peacock pheasant's call sounds like a well-accentuated, " That's enough, that's enough! "

*   *   *   *

I had been reminiscing the events of the dry February when New Frog and I had watched the many pigs on the Mae Salak which had ended in an unforgettable encounter with a big boar. Both the boar and February seemed very remote as I peered out of the little field hut in the middle of an abandoned opium field. The rain drizzled down endlessly, and high on Doi Vieng's south slope it was cold. We were having great difficulty in keeping the campfire going as we tried to dry out our gear. For three days since the long climb we had met this deluge. Doi Vieng was no place in the middle of the rains.

A rare blood-red orchid was reported to be in bloom just at this time. I wanted to collect a few specimens in addition to the many other species of *Vanda* which bloom during the month of August on Doi Vieng. There was also a likely possibility that we might find gaur and tiger. In any case, it was again the challenge of Doi Vieng; here on this great, bleak mountain a hunter's luck was like that of the deep-sea fisherman—you could never be sure what you might run into.

Big Pig stood up, stretched and dislodged a load of water from the leaf roof above him. He swore loudly at the rain, but made no effort to remove his soaking shirt.

" Any man that's out in this plague-stricken weather is either a fool or his father was a crocodile," he said bitterly.

" One more day and we will go sliding back down that

trail," I replied, feeling just as disappointed with the weather. Orchid or no, I was beginning to feel that we should all be back at home again, where a man could settle by a cosy hearth and feel dry again.

A long cry from a human voice far up the slope startled us so that no one bothered to answer for a few moments. Then Big Pig, gazing incredulously up the slope, whooped several times in the Lahu fashion. The voice came back, sounding very desperate, and this time we could make out that the man was trying to summon assistance. Whoever it was had probably glimpsed our smoke and guessed that other men chanced to be around. We were all trying hard to believe that anybody else would be around in that weather.

" Little Pig, you and Gets Lost go up and find out what the trouble might be," Big Pig ordered. " But be careful it might be a trick by some lost bandits, or it might even turn out to be some ghosts! "

Little Pig picked up my 30/30 rifle and trudged off up the hill with Gets Lost trailing behind. Some fifteen minutes later, I could see the shapes of three men coming through the hazy mists and the lead man carried a heavy burden on his back. Gets Lost, carrying a man pick-a-back came thudding down the steep trail and called ahead to us to make way for a badly wounded man. " A wild boar has gotten this poor Lahu," he said panting heavily and placing his burden gently onto the raised bamboo floor of the hut.

" Wild boar! " the other stranger half shouted, " My brother is nearly dead from having met a wild boar." He placed two muzzle-loaders against the hut, one of them belonging to his companion. He looked completely exhausted, but he had hung on to both guns as well as carrying the wounded man.

The men helped me stretch the patient out on his stomach, and because the light was very poor, I had Little Pig light up some faggots of pitch pine. When I had removed the man's wet and torn homespuns, what a wild boar could be capable of met our appalled stares. The worst of these wounds were across the man's back, several of them longer than a foot in length. The skin over the right ribcase was in ribbons, exposing the ribs, which fortunately had not been broken. The muscles of his right thigh had been deeply cut, and I was again shocked to see that the wounds were full of debris. Most of the bleeding had stopped and I placed a clamp on a vein that still bled. Since the bear-mauling case I had seen during the previous year, I carried a fairly complete medical kit. It now came in very handy, and before I was through with my patient some five hours later, I felt that I was really a surgeon after all, although the professional man would have been horrified had he seen my work.

The man was in such pain that after debating with myself, I gave him an injection of morphine* which calmed him considerably. He bore through the emergency activities that followed with incredible bravery even though I had no anaesthetics. The morphine, at best, served to reduce the terrible pain, but he was not under real sedation. When I ran out of regular sutures, we resorted to using ordinary thread which Little Pig boiled and handed to me. I left the larger wounds open at one end to allow drainage, feeling more like a seamstress than a surgeon. With a great deal of trouble, I managed in the end to dress each of the many wounds, having first to clean out the collected foreign material. I believe that even a real surgeon might have wept had the patient been admitted in a well-equipped hospital. The nearest hospital was five days of hard walking without heavy loads. The best chance for my patient rested in doing what we could right there in the field hut. He needed a transfusion desperately, and I was quite cer-

---

* Purchase of almost any drug, including medical morphine and available antibiotics, was legal on the open market without doctor's prescription in Thailand during those years.

tain that he would be dead by morning. In addition to the hundreds of stitches I had made, I used up a roll of adhesive to make " butterfly " sutures for the smaller wounds. I wound up my ministrations by giving the man a shot of penicillin, then collapsed on my sleeping bag completely exhausted.

Mountain men must be indestructible where others might succumb. The man's groans throughout the night were actually reassuring, and at least one or two men sat by him to comfort him through his ordeal. We were all in great spirits the next morning because we felt that we had won. The patient even smiled a few times and told me touchingly that he had appreciated our efforts.

The outcome of it all was that our patient made it. Five days later we helped to carry him back to his village where he shows the numerous scars rather proudly to this day. He will never know how proud and happy it made the amateur medic who worked on his wounds.

While the man had been recovering in the hut, his companion took Big Pig, Little Pig and myself to the place where the boar had been met. This was at noon on the second day after our patient had arrived and the rains had stopped. After much discussion, we all agreed that the boar ought to be hunted just on the principle of his having mutilated a fellow human being. I was not greatly enthused about the dubious justice involved because the boar had probably attacked in all his right to do so, and he was not a habitual killer that would be meeting men frequently. My Lahu companions thought quite differently, feeling that it was appropriate to seek revenge for a fellow man. The chase certainly had the promise of much excitement, and I would have welcomed it had not the memories of the big Mae Salak boar been so fresh. It was definitely risky, but I was as foolish as the Lahus. Secretly I hoped that another charging boar would not put me through a cold sweat like the last one.

The man who guided us to the spot was named "Kha Pa" (Gets Stuck) and his companion was called "Aw Neh" (Soft Rice). These were Lahus of the southern group, and although they went by names which were no less ludicrous than my more northerly companions, Little Pig commented quite a few times that, "These folks have very funny names!"

Gets Stuck took us to the top of the main ridge of Doi Vieng and down a long slope to the head of a stream where the broomgrass was thick. These grass patches marked ancient opium fields made by Meo tribesmen some forty years before. It was hazardous country in which to hunt wild pig, and there were few game trials here. My better judgement told me to give up this useless retaliation on a boar which would probably never harm another man as long as it was left alone.

"Over there by that small gooseberry tree," Gets Stuck said pointing across the shallow valley. "Soft Rice heard the boar snorting above him as he tracked a sambar buck through that grass when he surprised the boar. His gun missed fire and before he could move away the boar had him down." I had heard the details before and pictured the man as he hunched over, exposing his back to the boar. The boar had lost interest after Soft Rice fainted from the many strikes. Gets Stuck had worked his way over to his companion from above and found him bleeding and abandoned by the boar. He had risked being charged himself to rescue the man, but the boar had moved away down the valley by the time he reached his friend. Then with tremendous effort, he had carried the wounded man up the slope in the drizzling rain and almost to our camp.

The story was vividly in mind now, but where in all that formidable grassland would the boar be today. I turned to Little Pig, the "one-who-thinks-like-an-animal" and asked for his opinion. He stood there for a moment studying the terrain before us, then he asked Gets Stuck, who had hunted this section before, to tell him where the boar usually bedded. Gets Stuck was not at all sure. So Little Pig, thinking like a boar, pointed to a section of grass just below some rocky outcroppings and said, " There, that's where I would bed if I were the boar!" And of course he was right. His sharp eyes had seen what later turned out to be an old nest even from where we stood, some two hundred yards on the opposite side of the valley.

As we circled above and towards the rocks, Little Pig stopped again to look at some old tracks. We all looked expectantly at our little wizard, for whom even Big Pig had profound respect, and waited for his further opinions.

" I take the old nest to be last year's, and it must belong to the same boar because there are no tracks of other pigs here. This year, that boar nests in another spot, right up there," he explained as though he had known this par- ticular boar all his life. " He just *has* to go over there and make a new nest, don't you see? " I did not see and thought that he was being too sure of himself over a most unpredict- able thing. His further explanations confused me even more, although Big Pig was nodding his head in complete agreement. This was a fantastic description involving the movements of ticks in relation to the direction of wind and rain, so that the boar would choose a special direction to escape them. When it came to jungle knowledge, Little Pig was a triple " Ph.D."

" Yes, they'll do it every time," he said with glee, and would have rushed right out to the spot to prove that he was right. I insisted that we should sit down and plan the approach very carefully on the assumption that Little Pig's theories were correct. I respected his predictions of animal movements with deep awe, but I had every intention to plan the hunt as carefully as possible. I wanted to take advantage of every possible point in our favour so that we would be taking the minimum risks. Soft Rice's mis- fortunes were too fresh in my mind.

"We will skirt that broomgrass from above," I said, "and try to get the boar up by throwing stones into it from positions on those rocks." It was the only practical approach, yet it still involved considerable blind travel through the tall grass, something I wanted to avoid.

To gain the short rocky ridge above the place where we thought the boar might be lying, it was necessary first to push through some thorny brambles and bracken ferns. The ground was hard here and very slippery from a rain-soaked covering of mossy slime which clings to the ground in such places after heavy rains. It was difficult going and I found myself panting hard by the time we reached half-way up the other slope. I came to an abrupt halt behind Little Pig as he stooped to study some fresh tracks. Then he turned to me with a startled expression, almost of fear. He said, quite breathlessly, "Go back quickly and noiselessly the way we have come!" With that he half pushed me back down the slope, becoming more panicky with each step. Gets Stuck and Big Pig had paused further down and seemed to get the idea at once. I was still uncertain what had caused Little Pig's strange behaviour, and thought that he might have seen what to him was some evil spiritual omen. I stopped and asked him what it was all about.

"We nearly walked into the boar, Jaw Maw. His tracks crossed the trail just there, so fresh that I could *smell* him!" Catching his breath again he added, "The boar knows we are after him and he is *hunting us* even now ... Get out of here quick!"

A large rock to our right which I had marked earlier loomed out of the tall grass some fifty yards away. It looked like a good refuge to make for, and the four of us now hurried towards it. Little Pig's announcement had us in a state of controlled panic and I thought that it was a little ridiculous. But when a Lahu looks frightened, he usually has good reasons. I hurried along and soon realised that the Lahus were all making much better time than I was, and they were not going to wait for me. I felt like calling " Wait for me ! " then again felt that we were looking like fools fleeing from nothing. An ominous silence closed around me as I paused, determined now that I had no reason to panic or run. Slowly I stepped out into less dense brackens and grass, keeping my eyes behind me. When I had gotten about fifteen feet beyond the thick grass, I paused and faced back the way we had come. Little Pig was already up on the rock beckoning to me to come. I motioned to him that I would join him in a little while, and felt relieved now that I had better visibility. I eyed a twisted oak to my right and wondered if I should try to climb it. I heard no noise and again was certain the boar was not deliberately hunting us just then.

I was taking cautious steps towards the big rock when I heard a snort just to the left and above me in the grass. Then there was a sudden swishing of grass and a quick, choppy inhaled-exhaled coughing as the boar launched into a crashing charge. Until then, he had actually been stalking me, just as Little Pig feared, without making any noise. Some thirty yards above, he had probably followed a trail which was well known to him.

A sudden steadiness came over me like a warm glow for which I have no explanation. I had a relatively poor field of fire and should have had every doubt in the world that I could execute a good shot there. I raised my rifle and looked deliberately at the safety catch to see that it was off. Actually, I was probably so scared just then that I had no nerves left to contend with! If that was the case, then nature has made a wonderful provision. There was that sensation of being drunk and yet finding yourself steady and clear. I told myself, " One shot . . . remember to aim . . . aim very carefully . . .". I saw the boar's head break from the grass, still only partially visible, and I shot at once at the head. I could not miss him at five yards, but again, like my experience on Mae Salak, I had to remember that his momentum was going to carry him right onto me if I did not move. The strike of my bullet moved the charging boar for me, making him dip off to the right and to crash into the brackens a few yards to my right. I was still on my feet and could not suppress a desire to shout my victorious joy. My bullet had caught the boar neatly on the base of the snout and killed him instantly. This had buckled his front legs as he landed on them and threw him into a roll.

I was all nerves again after my joyous shout and the cheers from the three Lahus on the rock behind me. When they had reached me, I smoked nervously and stared at the trampled grass which marked the trail of the boar. Gradually, I got over it and experienced an odd feeling of wonderment. It all seemed like a vague dream that could not have happened at all.

Later, Little Pig thumbed the stained and jagged-edged tusks. " It has been broken before," he said. " These jagged ends explain the bad wounds on Soft Rice." He pulled out his skinning knife, smiling happily and began to remove the boar's testicles. " We don't want this meat to get ' fragrant ' do we? " he said laughing.

" Why was this boar so quick to follow us, Little Pig? "

" Jaw Maw, I can tell you that immediately," he said. " Come here and I will show you." He ran his hand over the boar's snout and showed me a number of black spots that covered much of the surface of the skin behind a flaring nose. Without even looking, this amazing jungle man might have known all along that there was a good example of a boar which had been in the rattan. The thorns from rattan roots had penetrated the boar's skin, working their way deeper into the tissues until the delicate membranes inside were being irritated. I was learning much from Little Pig.

He slapped his bloodied hand across the boar's snout and looked at me with a smile, " They are bad ones, Jaw Maw, the boars that come from the rattan."

CHAPTER SEVEN

Kings and their Domains

Veu da k'o neh a hpu; Na ta k'o sha a hpu—
Vui fa k'o vui a hpu; A fa k'o htaw la suh!

Dress well and you meet no girls;
Carry a gun and you see no game—
Watch for snakes and you don't find them;
Don't watch, and you die from its bite!

FOR several miles on every side of the steep mountain slopes, the partially cultivated tracts of wild tea contrasted like wide firebreaks with the darker forests at the edges. The white, delicate blossoms permeated the air with a faint fragrance, giving a hint of their identification in the family of Camelias. From the ridge where we stood, a haze of smoke could be seen hanging over the sunken valley where the hamlet lay, a mile or so up the cascading stream below. A slight chill still lingered, waiting for the rising sun to lift it together with the haze and the night's accumulation of dew from the lush terrain. The tops of the higher mountains ahead were shrouded in loose banks of mist clouds, already glowing at the far rims from the sun behind them.

It had been a good start. We had left the river an hour before dawn in order to take the long climb up the barren south slope of Doi Lang Ka before the sun's heat. The Shelleh chief who had spent the night at our camp had warned us that there was no water from the hamlet to the shallow saddle beyond the first peak, a good six hours' climb. I had tried to interest him in joining our hunting party, but his mission was of pressing importance. With his two grown sons squatting respectfully behind him, he had explained that the Chinese merchants in Chiengmai valued his collection of bear galls for medicine. These he would exchange for a good supply of aphrodisiac, and, if time permitted, search around the markets for a new hat, preferably the " long-lasting " (felt) kind, something that his people would admire and respect him for. The hat he was wearing " did not keep the hair in," and his newest wife had agreed to terms of marriage on a promise that he would get a new hat.

Other than the few Shelleh hunters who had gone there on occasions, Doi Lang Ka had few visitors. The mountain-living Thai farmers were mostly concerned with picking and cultivating wild tea. They also believed that ghosts roamed the tops of these ranges. Beyond the last tea clearings, there are no human trails, and Doi Lang Ka remains one of the most beautiful rain forests to the east of the Chiengmai valley—another Doi Vieng Pha. Here, the rare Barred-back pheasants are still to be found, and a conservation programme will continue as long as " ghosts " are reported there.

At the hamlet's spring, we filled our canteens and sat awhile to smoke. Several of the tea cultivators saw us and came towards us to investigate our suspiciously armed group. Big Pig, who did not love tea farmers, stood up, adjusted his pack on his shoulders and glared with annoyance at the approaching men.

" Let's be on the move before these people take all day asking silly questions," he said through his teeth with unnecessary hostility.

" *Pai nai, pai nai* (Where to?) " came the cheerful shouts as we began filing up the ridge.

" We look for ' phi ' (ghosts) on Lang Ka," New Soul yelled, typically mutilating the Kham Muang in Lahu fashion. The men stopped, looking at us in wonder and shaking their heads. I waved to them and smiled. They waved back feebly, unsmiling.

Near the top of the first ridge, a number of game trails appeared and disappeared, making it easier to tramp through the thick brackens and grass. Once we were on the ridge itself it was like reaching an inhabited area again, with well-defined elephant trails marking the main route along the narrow razor back. A refreshing breeze from the southeast cooled our flushed faces and the call of barbets came as thrilling announcements that we were getting into the level of the *yeh* again. New Soul broke out in a Lahu lovesong, part of which was beautifully poetic sung in his clear tenor:

" The stag and the doe on the mountain's ridge,
The pair of quail in the woodland flat—
All creatures wild have a place to go,
But this child can find no resting place—
Shine like the sparkling cool spring,
Shine like the fragrant bohenia blossoms—
Give this child a place to end his search,
Instead of hard stones let his head rest
Upon the soft maiden's breast—oh-oh-oh-oh!

The second part of his song got somewhat out of hand, with New Soul's own improvisations drifting from the traditional into an unlikely description of mountain love-making and ending in an agonised " oh-oh-oh-oh . . ." At such a point he ended abruptly to point to the left, and his sudden exclamation to " Stop " made me turn to look back.

" There's your dream maiden, New Soul," Little Pig said pointing and backing away from the direction of his gaze.

Stepping back to where Little Pig stood I saw the big snake which was a pile of dark coils lying on a flat rock. The king cobra had raised its head about two feet, hood spread, and watched us steadily from about ten yards. Through the sparse bushes I could see the lighter colour of its throat and the wide, flat head exactly level and at right angles to the rising column of the neck. It was a large specimen of the Black or Melanistic phase of the king cobra* which are more common in the northern hills than are the common, brown-to-greenish forms. The shiny blackness stood out clearly on this serpent and a distinct hissing, human-like, could be heard as the head rose steadily.

I brought my rifle up slowly and at the same time saw Big Pig searching about beside me for a stone. When I had lined the cobra's head up in my sights, I felt Big Pig's hand on my elbow.

"Wait! Don't shoot or we will scare the game," he muttered.

I lowered my rifle and because the serpent did not move, thought that we had become unnecessarily alarmed. It was a fascinating sight which I wanted to watch for a few moments longer, so it was I who now stayed Big Pig's hand when he was about to throw the large stone that he had found. I slung my rifle again and began fishing in my kit bag for my camera while the big snake remained motionless, staring at us through beady eyes.

Suddenly the cobra jerked, raising his head another foot, and without further warning slithered off the rock and came towards us. It came to within some ten feet of us and raised up again, all in one smooth, incredibly fast motion. Big Pig released his rock and New Soul's shotgun went off with a roar, both men missing the raised head

---

* The author at the time of this experience did not have the deep interest in herpetology that he has today, and simply considered this species of snake to be a melanistic king cobra. However, as this volume goes to my publisher, there is reason to believe that we have here an entirely new species, possibly genus, of cobra. Scientific description of this serpent awaits the collection of specimens from which to make accurate analysis. From a badly mutilated young specimen, the author, at this point concludes that this snake is probably neither of genera *Naja* or *Dendraspis* (Taylor). It is likely that with some further research, we will have been speaking of the world's largest venomous serpent, discovered newly from the mountains of Thailand.

which did not even flinch. My moment's fascination turned immediately into an anxiety which is difficult to describe. I had a sickening feeling of having underestimated the serpent terribly—gambled unnecessarily and lost. I had a picture of the tea farmer shaking his head.

New Soul was reloading, quite unperturbed, saving the buckshot in the left barrel instead of using it. My own weapon was by now in my hands and I raised it. Big Pig had pulled his long knife and had it extended in front of him. One second I was looking at the cobra's raised head, and in the next the space where it had been was a blank. Over to the left, I saw the last of its tail disappear into the grass and checked myself just in time before firing uselessly at it. In another astounding flash of action, the cobra was on the trail behind us shooting its head up and emitting loud hisses. This time I took steady aim and fired into the hood just below the head, and the coils erupted into a springing and writhing mass on the trail. We stood back for a few moments then went over to see the big snake, an eighteen-footer.

It was the first time since I had been in Thailand that a king cobra had shown what I believe was real interest in attacking. Had it been the only time, I would have continued to be baffled as to why that particular individual had not just remained on the rock or slithered away from us. Before that day and since that day, I have seen a good many king cobras, most of them being of the more common olive-to-brown varieties. Most of them have moved hastily away, and I subscribe to the experts' opinions that the aggressive nature of the king cobra is vastly exaggerated. But I also subscribe to the belief that they are among the most unpredictable creatures in the jungles, and especially aggressive during mating seasons. Their tactics when angered, and their capabilities to introduce super-lethal doses of neurotoxic venom, make them to my way of thinking the most fearsome creatures that roam the forests. In my experience the king cobra has not shown what might be described as a " norm " for this species. Their behaviour was always surprising, and I believe firmly that much has to do with individual temperaments. They are as shy and elusive as any reptile I know, or they are extremely aggressive. I am no longer baffled at king cobra behaviour, not because I have learned all their secrets, but because I accept them as peculiar and unpredictable creatures.

And so, announcing all of our intentions to the herd of gaur on Doi Lang Ka, we continued up into the dark timberline above us, commenting more than once that we did not care to meet " big black snakes " again. But the " evil spirits " which were believed to live on this range were actually in the form of king cobras. It turned out to be a regular domain of this great serpent. And they were real kings. I shall always respect the month of May when the king cobras are busy with the business of mating and nesting. As the Lahu say, this is a time to " keep one eye open for flashing scales."

We camped that night in the main saddle of the two highest peaks of Doi Lang Ka. Here giant trees laden with ferns and orchids formed a high canopy over us, and the spring which came out from the roots of a great banyan supplied the sweetest and coolest water that can be found. At night, tree civets and giant flying squirrels sprang about in the banyan, which was in full fruit, and we were not bothered by the ants because all of them had moved over to attack the fallen fruit. The best possible omen for good hunting had been shown us—the appearance of a snake which is successfully killed. Little Pig was sure that it meant gaur on the following morning. There was no need to hurry out; it was sure as Na Law's love for him, Little Pig said. The rest of us concluded therefore, that we could not be sure. Na Law had at least eleven lovers that we could recall.

The dawn brought on a din of voices in the banyan tree, its branches heavy with bright, golden clusters of fruit. Birds and squirrels worked busily through the foliage, making the branches spring and shake, and a thousand voices seemed to blend in a naturally ordered orchestra. Like woodwinds, Whistling Barbets and Fruit Pigeons took up the melody and theme. Among these was the most beautiful voice in the jungles, the Whistling Green Pigeon, which carries a full solo, complicated yet perfect to eighth notes. The background chorus from hundreds of small throats resembling flutes, picalloes, and violins, came from Bulbul, Fairy Bluebirds, Hill Mynahs, Barbets, Thrushes, Jungle Magpies, Parakeets, and numerous other fruit-eating birds. More distinctly like violins, the continuous din from cicadas added special undertones. There was also a strong bass section taken up with just the right emphasis by the deep "Whoo-oop, whoo-oop" of Imperial Fruit Pigeons and the occasional deep squawk-and-growl of the Great Hornbills. Beyond the orchestra's stage the periodic whooping of gibbon apes rose in crescendos, lending what seemed an important part to the chorus. At times a hawk would swoop down into the many birds, and like a command from the maestro's baton, the music stopped, though briefly, then continued throughout the busy feeding hours of the morning.

I looked at the big Hornbill (*Buceros bicornis*), cocking his head from side to side in search of banyan fruit. The black streak just at the forward base of the " horn " indicated that it was a male. They were all male birds, I realised, because the females would be molted naked at that time of year, sitting in plastered-in tree hollows over equally naked fledglings. Without the male bird's dutiful support, these helpless ones in the nests would perish. I sat back against a tree and chuckled to myself at the thoughts I recalled concerning the Great Hornbills.

About two years before I had spent some time with the Lahus of Nam Ngai village, far to the west from where we then camped. One evening a young man came back from the fields carrying a male Hornbill with its huge beak hooked through the string of his crossbow. It was the nesting season, and I was saddened to think of the tragedy that the bird's death meant for some unfortunate female and its young. But the incident became a personal triumph for me instead and surely saved a number of Hornbills. It is one of those rather dishonest things I have done in my life of which I am very proud.

That evening I sat with most of the elders from that village, and we discussed various problems that had been outstanding in the village. I listened to them for several hours, then offered my opinions. " All hill people have these problems," I said solemnly, " and there is a good reason for them, especially matters such as loose behaviour among your young people." Then I introduced the idea of shooting male Hornbills during nesting season. Wasn't this sure to invite the wrath of evil spirits when the females screamed out in the agonies of starvation because the male bird could not supply food to opened beaks? I have never seen more intensely sober faces. Three " paw hkus " seconded my suggestion and declared them very timely wisdom. All of the elders agreed and it became Lahu law that night: no more hornbills would be shot during nesting season! The " taboo " later spread to many of the other tribal villages including, Shelleh, Lisu and Karen. A year later I asked a young Lahu from a village fifty miles south of Na Ngai to go out and shoot a Hornbill for me in the month of June, well beyond the nesting season. I got the reaction that I had been hoping for: " Oh no! " he announced loudly so that all the people could see that he was a law-abiding young man, " We hill-people cannot do that or leopards will come in to steal our pigs! "

The big bird above me cocked his head awkwardly at me and it made me feel very good to know that we were good friends. I thought I caught the faintest indication of a wink from his heavily-lashed eye just before he left the branch in a loud fanning of his great wings. His craw filled with banyan fruit, he banked in and out of the tall trees towards the sheer hills beyond where a mate had been carefully hidden.

About two miles to the north of camp, Big Pig and I climbed out on a rocky outcropping to have a look at the terrain below us. We had seen gaur tracks on the ridge just above camp, but these had been several days old and for some reason the animals had moved to the west where natural pastures were very poor. Fresh bear tracks now took our interest. Several oaks near us had been used for nests; and the upturned leaves from broken branches stood out in a silvery contrast to the dark green of undisturbed portions of the trees. It was difficult to determine which direction the bear had taken because the grass and weeds were matted and criss-crossed with their trails.

Below the outcropping, the grass-covered slope continued for about a hundred yards, disappearing into low scrubby jungle with dense rattan just beyond the rim of the brush. Beyond the billowing green of the jungles, we had what seemed a hundred miles of visibility, as far as the hills of Nan to the east. Some thirty miles to the southeast were the nearest hill tribes, Shellehs, whose freshly-hoed rice fields stood out as red patches on the sides of another mountain range. I watched a Great Fishing Eagle (*Haliaetus leucoryphus*) soar through the saddle from the direction of our camp and head northeast. He raised his creamy head to look back over his left wing at the two man-things on the rocks, ruddered his white-barred tail to bank slightly in our direction, then kept on his long course for the Mekhong river ninety miles away. He was as much a stranger to these hills as we.

The brush below us heaved violently just to our left and out scampered two pine martins. With high-pitched, agitated squeals, they ran back and forth in the grass, keeping their attention towards the brush from which they had emerged. Then they came loping towards us excitedly, making for the high rocks upon which we sat. When they suddenly came upon Big Pig and me, the two martins experienced another shock and went squealing frantically off to the right to take immediately into the trees there. Big Pig and I smiled at each other and leaned forward to watch the brush again.

Soon Big Pig's hand came up and I followed the pointed finger to where the grass was moving gently in a long wake, exposing little flashes of black between the parted blades. I thought at first with amazement that it must be some new kind of black python until I saw the head rise and a flattening of the throat. It was just as incredible to be looking at another big black king cobra within the short time since we had seen the first one. For me, it was an uncommon thing to see even one of these big snakes, and yet this one together with another we were to encounter on Doi Lang Ka was to make this a most unusual trip for us. The name later given by the Lahu for this mountain was certainly justified, *Vui Na Hkaw* or "Black Snake Mountain." I would spend a hundred days or more in the jungles before seeing another black king cobra again.

The big serpent, easily as large as the one I had killed earlier, moved around in the grass where the martins had pranced about, raising and lowering its head until satisfied that the potential egg robbers had gone. Then it glided slowly back into the brush, while Big Pig and I watched in fascination. We told each other that we had not intended to go in that direction anyway and later in camp, told each of the other men to avoid the spot as though a bomb had been planted there. Before we left the rocks, we saw the big snake climb into the top of some low bushes and settle down to a morning's sun basking. We guessed that it might be the male cobra keeping guard over a female with eggs nearby. He was king of that particular sector and we did not care to interfere with his type of administration.

Some years later, I learned that the " King's " system of rule featured some very strange laws. If it were not for the male king cobra, the jungles would undoubtedly become infested with these fierce and deadly creatures. The reason for his jealous guarding of the female's eggs is quite contrary to common beliefs. He is one father who does not intend that his children grow up, simply because *he is extremely fond of eating the babies*! As the worst enemy of his own kind, the male king cobra guards seriously what to him is a delightful orgy as soon as the babies hatch, thus contributing most effectively to the control in balance of king cobra populations. Herpetologist friends have informed me that they have always had difficulties in collecting specimens of young king cobras and as far as I know, no one has collected a specimen of the black form, if this is indeed simply a black form of the better-known king cobra. There is probably very good reason for this. The only specimen of the common king cobra that I was lucky enough to collect came from the stomach of an adult male. This is probably not always the case, but I believe that cannibalism of the young cobras occurs whenever the female is unable to hide her eggs from the male king cobra. This is likely to be more often than not the case where the big black form of the mountains is concerned. It is also likely that for every male king cobra killed by man while guarding eggs, man unwittingly increases his chances of meeting other cobras by a considerable amount, since the king cobras apparently do not eat each other after maturity. The king cobra is a strictly cannibalistic snake; few other snakes will be found in an area inhabited by them, including pythons, the young of which are often eaten by king cobras. Little Pig tells of a large cobra he once killed which had swallowed a python nearly six feet long!

When Big Pig and I returned to camp about noon, we had brought with us as much of a young sambar buck as we could carry. With snakes still on my mind, I dumped my load of meat down onto banana leaves that New Soul placed near the spring, and looked around at the men we had left in camp, surprised that the general hum of conversation was also about some snake.

"Now don't tell me," I said half jokingly, "a big *vui na* came crawling into camp while we were gone?"

"No we didn't see *vui na*," New Soul answered, "but what do you think of a man like Little Pig who is so careless as to get bitten by a green viper!" They were all laughing, including Little Pig who sat over by the fire looking quite unruffled. When he got up and went over to where the dead snake was, I noticed that he had a slight limp.

I was astounded: Little Pig picked up what represented about the maximum sized Emerald Viper (*Trimeresurus*) as found in those parts. Normally no more than two to three feet in length, the specimen that had bitten him solidly on the top of his left foot was a good four feet long and two inches thick. It would have made most men very sick, but this little man, like several of his colleagues, was fortunately quite immune to its venom.

"These things have hooked into my flesh at least ten times," Little Pig announced proudly. He toyed with the wicked-looking serpent, showing me the long fangs and almost getting pricked by them in the process. I recalled other cases where the patient had swollen limbs twice and three times normal size, and usually with serious secondary infections.

"I didn't cut the wound like you said, Jaw Maw. Just squeezed it good, and you should have seen the 'juice' come oozing back out!" He thought this was very funny and laughed again because he imagined that I needed humouring.

"Little Pig is tough as a wild pig, and all pigs are used to viper bites," Gems concluded with what was excellent joking form for Lahus. For this he received a smart kick to his rear from Little Pig's snake-bitten foot. He leaped away laughing.

"Be careful, Little Pig," he called back, "you're liable to get snake juice all over my nice clothes!" Little Pig had pulled his skinning knife and began working on the sambar shoulder, a very "sick" man. He was not just fortunately immune to this particular snake, but he was an extraordinarily tough man. I watched in continued wonder at the lithe and muscular mountain man and was reminded of a small tiger in excellent condition.

That evening after a fine venison feast, we sat around a blazing fire and Big Pig officially dubbed the place "*Vui Na Hk'aw.*" As far as the Lahu are concerned, Doi Lang Ka has a number of important features, named as a result of that first trip. There's "Snakebite Camp," "Eagle Pass," "Stubbed Toe Ridge" (Gems on the way up the first day) and not in the least, "See-snake-again-Valley." The latter is an invention by the joint committee of Big Pig, Little Pig, and New Soul, and as a result of what certainly was my most terrifying experience with a King Cobra.

By the end of a week our exploration of Doi Lang Ka had been completed, and we knew where to find two rare animals that could have been most profitable if captured alive. These were Clouded Leopard and Barred-back Pheasant. Dealers all over the world wanted them, but they were as unlucky about obtaining them through our efforts as we were in the attempts to capture these shy creatures. They still roam freely in the rather impossible denseness of Doi Lang Ka. I hope it will always remain a haven for these rare and exotic animals.

On the second day after Little Pig had been bitten by

the viper, and just when we made first contacts with the fabulous Barred-back Pheasants, I happened to be coming up one of the long ridges to the west of our camp with the young brother of Gems who had joined our trip for the first time. We had been no more than a mile from camp, trying to find out something about the habits of the strange pheasants, when we ran into a very large troupe of Pigtailed Macaques. It appeared to me that all the monkeys were in the valley to my right, busily hunting for food in the treetops, and the two of us took no more than a passing glance at them as we walked slowly up the ridge.

Then a very small monkey, some fifty yards away from the main troupe, suddenly started screaming in the branches just over our heads, startled half out of its wits when it saw us. It raced through the branches towards the troupe only to find that it could not negotiate the distance between the tree that it had been playing in and the next one. Now its screams became as frantic as though it had gotten into the claws of an eagle, so that the boy, Ca Ti, and I had to exchange smiles over the absurd commotion the little fellow was creating over what was no danger at all. Our smiles played out very quickly when we realised all at once that the baby monkey's distress calls were not falling on heedless ears.

In a moment we were the victims of monkey misunderstanding. Alarming numbers of large male Pigtails were leaping through the trees towards us, coming, they imagined, to the aid of one of their young.

I had heard a number of stories about both Pigtails (nemestrina) and the Stump-tailed Macaque (speciosa) attacking hunters under unusual circumstances. These had happened to Lahu hunters armed only with a bow, or at best a muzzle-loading gun. In most cases the angered monkeys triumphed with ghastly results, finally tearing a man limb from limb. I had also seen a big male Pigtail once make quick work of five dogs, using its tremendous strength to grab a dog briefly while inflicting great slashes with its large canine teeth. My first reaction, therefore, was to join Ca Ti who was by then moving down the hill with the grace of a doe. But I realised that I was too late and had I tried to run, I would have been quickly overtaken.

In a loud chorus of throaty barks, the first of the big males reached me and hesitated, darting quick glances behind to see that more and more reinforcements were coming up. I knew that monkeys are something like dogs in that if a person shows fear or tries to retreat, the inevitable attack comes. In this case the monkeys could see that I was frightened, but paused because I had not retreated. I recall that about five big males were beginning to ring me in when I started shooting. I began by shooting a big boy just getting ready to spring off a bending bamboo which would have landed him right on me. Then I opened up as rapidly as I could until I had fired all six rounds from my rifle. It is probably most fortunate that I had had the sixth round in my chamber, which is not always my practice while hunting. It took six shots to even begin to turn the determined animals. Had I been trying to reload after my fifth shot, I am certain that the monkeys would have still pressed their attack at that point.

It was point-blank shooting and I could not miss. Six big males lay down quietly without apparently being noticed by the rest of the troupe. The sound of my rifle did not seem to frighten them at first, but with the diminishing raucous sounds from which the combined troupe gathered much courage, the monkeys began to retreat somewhat. I reloaded as quickly as I could, and managed to slip three more rounds from my pocket into my rifle before I had to work the first round quickly into my chamber and fire again. The seventh and eighth big males were the last that the leader, wherever he or she might have been, was willing to send into battle.

I still did not trust the monkeys not to attack again so stood where I had been standing, loading up again with my last round of ammunition (I always carry exactly ten rounds for luck!). Something told me that the fight was over, mainly because the dear little baby monkey which had started the whole thing had found a way out from its stranded position and joined mother.

I stood there for a few moments sweating hard and thought how very brave the monkeys had been. I did not feel sorry for the dead ones at first, because I knew what terrible intentions they had had for me. But like a stupid war where men must die uselessly over some misunderstanding, so had these magnificent jungle creatures. I had certainly not wanted to kill any of these animals, nor could I afford the ammunition, which was extremely difficult for me to obtain in those days. With the loss of eight fine males from the troupe, I thought at first I had been guilty of removing the best sires, but I watched twice that number of excellent males moving away slowly with the rest of the troupe about ten minutes later. It had been one of the largest groups of Pigtails I had seen, numbering at what I guessed to be close to a hundred monkeys. There would be, I felt, few other incidents when members of this huge troupe would give up their lives again under similar circumstances. Normally they would be avoiding man and tending busily to their search for food, with few other than the Clouded Leopard to snatch a member here and there while the troupe slept in the top of tall trees.

Like the courage which the attacking monkeys had gotten from the sound of each other's loud barking, my young Lahu friend Ca Ti took heart when he heard my rifle sounding off again and again. He soon came racing back up the hill to me, and because he was a Lahu son of a meat hunter, admired with joy the nice pile of meat that could now be had from the slain monkeys. For my part, I felt no joy just then, and wished that I had had the young lad's agility to have got away from the slaughter that I was forced to commit.

I spent all the next day in camp preparing study skins from some of the monkeys I had killed, and saving the skulls and skeletons of those I did not stuff. After the incident with the monkeys I made only one more long trip from our camp, with the thought furthest in my mind that again " Black Snake Mountain " would have for me another experience that I could never forget.

Little Pig chose to accompany me on that last outing from our camp. New Soul slapped his thigh with a resounding smack just before we left the camp and said that he had better come along to " carry the meat or carry Little Pig back," referring to the remote possibility that Little Pig might be snake-bitten again.

About a mile from camp we picked up fresh tracks of a large Sambar stag and Little Pig began " reading " tracks again. His opinion was that we would catch up with the stag in about two hours' time, that it would carry about two hundred kilograms of meat, weighed on the hoof about three hundred kilos (660 lbs.), limped for some reason, had a pretty good rack, was bothered by flies, and that it had just returned from a " poang " or mineral lick. When it came to reading tracks, Little Pig knew his stuff.

" Will he stand while I mount him to ride him back to camp? " New Soul asked with mock seriousness.

" No, he'll mount you instead, because I'm going to use you as a decoy fat doe which he will come running to see," Little Pig replied. " New Soul, why couldn't you have been a pretty maiden instead of being such a smelly, ugly old boar? "

" Little Pig, when I was leaving my mother's womb, legs first, I can remember hearing the people saying as they tugged on me, ' Ah, here comes the greatest gift women ever had! ' You know that, I know that, and so do all the girls."

" I have great regard for you, ' Older Brother ' and I feel very sad at times when I recall how the people had to pull on you to bring you into the world. It is unfortunate that your head became loosened, and even more unfortunate that you were not a girl!" Little Pig spat with amazing accuracy at a big spider in the middle of a web five feet across. It scrambled down and took cover under a leaf. My hand brushed the top of a nettle bush and made me spring back with a start. I looked back with a foolish expression at New Soul who controlled a laugh. Then with the tip of his long knife, he deftly flicked a small branch from the nettle and handling it very carefully by the stem, tossed it lightly onto Little Pig's exposed leg.

In a flash, Little Pig's long knife whipped around, slicing an imaginary enemy and he stood facing us in the classical sword-fighting pose. Just as quickly he noticed the nettle and the humour on New Soul's face.

" Why you misconceived child of your mother's whoring! You dare do that to Little Pig?" Without another word, he sat down and began laughing. I watched the two Lahus, amused mainly at the characteristic speed with which they, like all their people, flew into and out of anger. Their women were the same; they might be seen sobbing hysterically one minute then laughing the next.

The Sambar's tracks led around the base of a large, jutting boulder, crossed an open ridge, and went straight down the steep slope into a wooded ravine. He had walked in and out of the small brook for about fifty yards, browsing the soft grasses along the banks. We never found out what he had done after that because the Sambar suddenly became unimportant to us just at that place.

The king cobra, newly shed and looking very black and shiny, half fell from the lower branches of a bohenia tree. It landed with a thud about twenty feet above us, and like a runaway water hose came threading its way through the clumps of grass towards us. Coming from our left, it was heading right for me, middle man in our small file. The two Lahus broke away from me in opposite directions, Little Pig going downstream and New Soul sprinting back upstream. Both of them yelled to me to *Get out!*

One of the reasons why tramping the jungles will never pall is that a man will be faced with sudden and unexpected decisions that he must make for himself. Such decisions may or may not be the right ones despite long training and experience in the jungles. In my case, I have never been able to separate fright from thrill, and the two have a way of gripping me in such a way that I usually make the wrong decision when encountering dangerous wild creatures. If I say that I was frightened that morning, the actual emotion I had would be more properly and honestly expressed. But I recall a certain fascinated thrill which remains more vividly. For a few seconds it seemed unbelievable that the king cobra would show such magnificent and determined aggressiveness, or that he would choose to demonstrate his fierce intentions while I was watching. I I was thinking, " This couldn't be happening to me!" And because he did not succeed in killing me, I was left having gained a rare experience which I doubt will come my way again. My curiosity as to what might be expected of the king cobra is forever satisfied, and I have no desire to meet one again under those circumstances.

I might have escaped had I run as fast as I could after Little Pig. Still, the cobra might have continued his chase, or I might have stumbled on the slippery rocks in the stream. Things *might* have been worse. Right or wrong, I stayed where I had stopped, and as the cobra reached me, I swung the muzzle of my rifle at the rising head. For a split second, it seemed as though I could not sweep that head aside; it seemed to be following the rifle barrel closer and closer to me as the snake continued to extend its length towards me, powerfully and inexorably. It was not to be flipped to one side so easily. Because it had not risen to full maximum extension of its long sinuous column, the point of balance still lay solidly on the ground. I had to use all of my strength to push it to one side, but no sooner had I achieved this parry to the left than the head dipped out from my rifle muzzle and sprang up again at the original position. This time I swung with more force and struck the cobra on the neck, flattening it very briefly into the grass and sedge on the bank. Instead of trying to get a shot off, I continued to strike down with the barrel of my rifle, hitting the writhing neck a few times and managing to keep the head from rising again. Then I fired a round into the cobra with my rifle extended in both hands. The bullet struck just under the neck and lifted the head about a foot off the ground in a spray of dirt and pebbles. This managed to confuse the cobra and he turned away from me to regain his directions. In that second or two, I had a chance to take aim and fire a second round at the head as it moved searching for another opening from which to rise.

I stood there, trembling and sweating, and watched the snake writhing in death. Then I backed up the stream as the shiny loops of the cobra's body came tumbling down into the stream, its head in mangled shreds covered with dirt and sand. My two Lahu companions appeared moving cautiously along the right bank, and because they simply must, they were laughing with delight at the consternation my face showed when I turned to them. Little Pig's uncomplimentary observation was that I looked " as though I had just died." I was not at all amused at his humour this time.

" Why there are leeches in this stream! " New Soul said unexpectedly, " Let's get out of here and off of Doi Lang Ka and go see what the women and children are doing back home. This place has too many leeches even this time of the year! " Home was not exactly around the corner. It took three days of walking. And leeches were certainly not my reason to be leaving that mountain, nor would I be forgetting big, black snakes as easily as New Soul could.

CHAPTER EIGHT

Right and Left of the Trail

Te geh te k'o law; Te geh ca k'o meh.
Work together and the load is lighter;
Eat together and the food tastes better.

JUST above our camp I flicked a cigarette stub into the
Mae Khawng stream and watched it go bobbing along
over the gentle rapids. I wondered if that filtered tip
would hold up long enough to reach the roaring Salween
river, some eighty miles away and across the Thai border
in Burma, or whether some hungry fish would gobble it
down by mistake. In any case, anyone who saw that filter
tip would probably wonder what it was and where it
came from, because most of the people for the next five
hundred miles along this section of the river would be
seeing one for the first time. Such cigarettes were difficult
enough to obtain in Chiengmai then, and the remote spot
where that stub was introduced into the stream was an
unlikely place from which it might have been done. I could
be sure that I was the first man smoking a filter tip cigarette to come to that place in north-western Thailand. I felt
very privileged to have such an honour and it was a great
joy to be a happy intruder in such a place.

The big boar had gone up the same side of the stream
that I had chosen to take for a short hunt that evening. A
barking deer would have been a better choice, meeting the
needs of our small party of six with tastier meat, but we
did not know the country and I decided to follow the boar

anyway. We had come nearly thirty kilometres that day over very rough terrain from a midway camp between Mae Hongsorn and the Mae Khawng stream. My feet reminded me of this with each slow step I took and even the light, ·30/30 carbine I carried felt too heavy. I had no intentions of going very far, nor did I think that the boar would be far up the stream. By some good chance, I felt, he would conveniently oblige by standing near the bank at the next bend, rooting unconcernedly while I casually and without further exertions obtained meat for the gang.

It was the thrill of being in new country that soon allowed me to forget the aches and pains in my tired limbs. It was even easier to forget about tracking the boar when I was greeted at the next bend of the stream by the screech-ings and commotion of a family of otters. Stalking carefully up to the edge, I hid behind a large tree and sat down to watch the fun going on in the wide pool of still water.

The family numbered about twenty in all, having con-gregated at the pool to begin their evening fishing in earnest. I was reminded of a family reunion at the beach, with everybody dashing madly for the surf because the inland folks hadn't seen the ocean for years. The Big Daddy of the pack was obviously a national champ, and he cruised about mightily, impressing the " women and children " no end. He made long, deep dives and erupted out of the water with a good-sized fish every time. These he gobbled down with amazing dispatch on the same wide rock at the other bank. After about fifteen minutes, he seemed to be satisfied and began helping the females in the strenuous business of bringing half-stunned, smaller fish for the young otters. This was a task involving training as well as feeding. An adult otter nipped a newly-caught fish just hard enough to daze it so that the babies could chase and catch it after it was released in the shallows near them. This excited the young ones into frenzies of delight and relish; their high-pitched squeals and yaps resounded in the valley and their little bellies were rapidly becoming round and well filled with fish from what seemed an endless supply. The little ones seemed to be learning the art of gobbling down a fish in the rapid fashion of otters. It had to be learned slowly as the babies grew, perhaps because one just had to be able to eat a fish rapidly and artfully in order to be an otter. Always, one or two comical little fellows were taking too long over their meals, trying to decide whether to begin from the tail end or the head of the fish, growling fiercely not unlike a small kitten over a mouse. The whole spectacle would have made a wonderful motion picture.

After some time, the Big Daddy came up very fast from a long dive, chattering so loudly that all the heads were turned towards him. He had seen something down under a dark sunken log worth yelling about. Circling around a few times on the surface, he disappeared again under the log. I could see him faintly in the clear pool from my position some ten feet above on the bank. There was a lot of churning water and the mud was stirred into a reddish cloud around the log. It seemed for awhile that he had run into real trouble and that he was caught fast by something. When he finally surfaced again after an amazing long time, he seemed quite exhausted and made silently for the rock on the opposite bank. He had made me so curious that I stood up for a better view of what might have been the cause of Big Daddy's great battle under the log.

A long, dark shadow went gliding out downstream from the muddied area and looked at first like a phantom otter nearly twice the size of the big male otter which had attacked it. I recognised it only when I could see the white flecks which marked the fang and claw wounds on the back of the large fish. Big Daddy had been incredibly brave to attempt to take on a fish that large, and it was certainly not to his discredit that he could not handle it. Resembling somewhat the uncommon American Bowfin, the big " *pla sawn* " was one of the biggest of its kind that I had seen.

Almost too late, I realised that there went the meat for our dinner I had hoped to find. As the big river fish reached the shallow end of the pool just above the gentle rapids, its dorsal fins almost broke the surface and I took a quick shot at its head with my ·30/30. Otters forgotten, I ran down the bank to get ahead of the fish as it floated down into the rapids. Behind me, many otters screeched and dived into the water in what for them must have been a rude shock. Moments later, I had my fish which had been shot through the head. It was as nice a *pla sawn* as I have taken from even the larger rivers and must have weighed well over forty pounds, enough for the six of us with plenty to spare.

It had been one of those trips that Big Pig liked to call " exploring for new grazing grounds." My companions were all of them as keen to " see what was on the other side of next ridge " as I was. I had charted out a fairly reliable and well-known course to take as far as Mae Hongsorn from Chiengmai, then up the Muang Pai trail to the Mae Khawng. From there, we had the river to follow northeastward to its headwaters near the Burma border. The best maps to which I had access showed this portion of Thailand to be uninhabitated and predominated by various karst formations, with the higher mountains along the Burma border. It promised exciting new hunting grounds which we started out to find the next day with eager anticipation. We had plenty of time, enough rice to last more than ten days, and that wonderful feeling of abandoning all worldly cares which was replaced completely by the pleasures of exploration.

For the next six days we moved through rugged karstlands and knew something of the joy of living mostly off the land. Honey was abundant, and even that early in the season, we found enough jungle vegetables to keep every meal interesting and nourishing. Big Pig later liked to refer to that trip as " the time we ate only young meat," meaning that the game had been so plentiful that we had a choice of selecting out only young animals for their tender meat. It was a week for the jungle foods gourmet with a different dish of wild meat or vegetable at every meal, topped off with so much wild honey of superior flavour that not a few of us got somewhat ill from it at times. Despite it, New Soul, our bee expert, kept right on robbing every bee tree we came across and getting increasingly more sullen every day from the hundreds of stings he sustained. These would have killed anyone less than a relative of the bear which he admitted he was. He had acquired the nickname of " 'La-K'o " (Pine Marten) since he had been about seven years old and his method of attacking the honey bee was an art.

Like any good fighter, the whole process begins with the right attitude. New Soul would approach a bee tree not at all unlike a curious bear and " feel " the situation out. Some colonies being more aggressive than others, these approaches would often end in much swearing and dancing about. " You have to show the bees that you are not afraid of them," he would say, pulling the stingers from his nose and ears. When he had fired up his large tobacco pipe, he moved in again on the most aggressive bees and reversing the pipe, he would blow the tobacco smoke from the bowl through the stem, directing the jet of smoke directly into the bees. Certainly, the bees were to be pitied far more than New Soul at the end of such an operation. The brand of mountain tobacco he smoked was enough to get him five years in jail had he used it around civilised society. Then, with the bees rendered very sick or at best inaccurate in their attacks, he would enlarge the hole in the tree as needed to accommodate his hands for the big steal. It is said of New Soul that he is the greatest bee-fighter in all the hills and that in Hell he is destined to be punished by everlasting bee stinging. But as far as I could see, he took a good deal of his retribution through his earthly encounters with angry bees. After any such operation he would sit down for a while first to lick the dripping honey from his grimy fingers then to *shave* the hundreds of stingers away with his hunting knife. As immune as this hardy man was to bee and wasp stings alike, he still braved considerable pain after a few hundred stings had been registered. Up to fifty stings, he told me, were quite unnoticeable.

On the morning after the sixth night through this great wilderness area, we were all amazed to find human footprints again. From the top of one of the higher passes, we had the impression that there would be no human habitation within the distance of another five or six days' travel through the karst and rain forest areas ahead. We had not seen a single highland field clearing as far as the blue mountains which mark the north-south cordillera of the Sam Muen complex. From that range on, we knew that there would be hill tribes and that the main Fang-Chiengmai motor road lay only a few days' journey beyond. We studied the bare foot prints in the sand along a small stream, and decided that whatever hillmen had made them must be living within a day's hike from the spot. They could have been hunters from a tribe that none of us knew, or members of the wild and strictly nomadic Phi Tong Luang.

When we had gained the ridge above the stream, we followed it for a few miles along old wild elephant trails. With most of my attention upon the terrain ahead, I blundered into the middle of a warrior wasp " perimeter " and realised my mistake just seconds short of disaster. Usually, there is fair warning by the "sentries" of these giant wasps which take up positions on a wide perimeter, sometimes as far as fifty yards from the nest. I was jarred to horrified realisation of my error by a dull roar which came from under the ground practically at my feet. Then a lone sentry rose up from a blade of thatchgrass and buzzed wicked warning that we had trespassed into forbidden grounds. We all obeyed most humbly and crouching low to the grass made hasty retreat until the wasp stopped following our group. Then we sat down for a break and to breathe relief that none of us were groaning and nursing painful stings. My Lahus were simply delighted that we had found a wasp nest and several of them suggested that we should make camp nearby so that the larvae could be taken that night.

To the Lahu and all of their related mountain tribesmen, no delicacy is more important that the larvae of the warrior wasp. There are more inter-tribal conflicts resulting from misunderstanding of ownership or flagrant robbery of another's claim to a wasp colony than from any other cause. These are their most prized delicacy, and one large colony represents a great wealth to any family who can make exclusive claim and exploit the "gold mine". The young wasps, when properly prepared, taste like some delicate seafood. Men and boys spend many days tracking the wasps which have come to bait. These are made more easily visible by attaching a light white feather to the busy worker as it carves out a bit of meat to carry home. When a source or colony is found, tribesmen blaze a few trees in the vicinity, and attach various symbols made from bamboos to indicate that the location had been claimed and is only awaiting maturity.

The actual operation of taking the larvae is done at night and with the aid of numerous firebrands. The strictly diurnal wasps cannot see at night, and stings from them are by chance contacts during the turmoil of the digging and removing of the five- and six-feet wide combs containing the larvae. Even then, a number of men may come home with very painful wounds.

The warrior wasp or hornet develops underground hives

which are spherical and up to eight feet in diameter. The earth which is removed from the huge burrows can often be seen from long distances in more open terrain. The individual workers are about two inches long and as thick as a man's finger. Aside from the economic importance which hill people attach to these insects, they must be said to be one of the real dangers of the higher ranges as far as man is concerned. A man needs to be only a bit more careless than I was that morning to meet with at least very great pain or even death in more unusual cases from multiple stings. The largest nests will have many sentries ringing the area and are usually quickly sighted. Smaller colonies may not be noticed until one stands right over it. When real alarm has been sounded, he would be lucky to get away with less than a dozen stings, enough to present the average man with a serious bid for his life. Not a few tribal children have been reportedly killed from three and four stings, and I am personally familiar with the case of a Lahu man who died in 1957 from only nine stings. One sting in my right thigh once incapacitated me for several days.

It did not take long for New Soul and Little Pig to discover that the colony we blundered into had been claimed by tribesmen, probably the same men whose tracks we had seen in the stream. This came as a big disappointment to the Lahus and there were many dejected comments as we manoeuvred carefully around the wasp area to move on up the ridge. At the top, we found other blaze marks on the trees and followed the occasional slashes until we came onto a discernible trail. By late afternoon, we were on a fairly well-used trail which followed various ridge lines. These were covered with virgin forests from which we could get only occasional glimpses of the deeply forested hills on both sides. We were coming into the newly established village on the east side of a slope almost before we realised it. All this had been hidden from our view because the village and the several opium poppy fields around it were on the far side of the range.

The previous November had seen the clearing of the new fields, and when the poppies were well established, the people had moved into the new site and were still in the process of finishing some of the dwellings. We had first to go through a field in full bloom and in the first stages of pod-cutting to start the raw sap of opium. Our first very startled discoverers were a group of Red Lahu women who were tending the matured poppy pods. We were as surprised to find Red Lahus in the area as the women were horrified at the sight of our motley presentation. My terrible appearance, with a week's beard, battered hat, and the fact that I was obviously non-Lahu was of no help. Our lovely ladies in their colourful red, black and white tribal colours began screaming and charging away towards the field hut while my Lahu men shouted and cheered them on.

Almost immediately, a stalwart male, armed with an enormous muzzle-loader, appeared at the hut's front, still groggy from the nap he had been taking while the women worked in the field. Without any questions, he raised the weapon, primed it, and got ready to fire one shot before drawing his sword and fighting to the death. Big Pig's cheerful greeting stopped him just in time.

"Ah, Friends and Cousins! Why be in such agitation to kill off your few remaining Lahu cousins?" He waved his Lahu bag at them to prove his identity.

"Never saw you all before, but you speak in Lahu words," said Friend with the big gun and the still suspicious glare.

"Lower your great gun, Cousin, before you waste a good load of powder and burn my only pair of pants," Big Pig retorted, the very cheerful tones mingled with laughter.

"Then state your purpose to scare my women," Cousin said in not exactly friendly gutturals.

" Women? Were those women? What difference do women make? Do you people worship women around here or something? " Big Pig pretended exasperation as he continued walking right on up to the hut. Then he announced, " Cousin, prepare to be honoured by our sudden visit and take us to your chief! "

Without taking his eyes off the apparition which was me, the man simply ignored Big Pig's request and sat down to continue the staring contest which had started between the two of us. Then I handed him my best smile and began speaking to him in the best Red Lahu accents that I then knew. I noticed that the several amulets he wore around his neck included the claw of the Golden Cat, signifying that he was a hunter of considerable accomplishment.

" We have not come to buy your opium or to look at your women," I continued, "and we meet only because you people have planted a new village on the trails of hunters."

"Ah, ' Meu Neu ' Lahu," he said, smiling for the first time and startling me with the distinction he made in Big Pig's and my Lahu-na speech.

" No, Ah-meh-li-ka people," Big Pig corrected quickly.

"Ah-meh-li-ka people? "

"Ah-meh-li-ka people."

" The very-Good-Guns-Making people? "

" Right, Brother."

" The Flying Machine-Making people? "

" Yes, and where they given birth to *Ka-la-hpu* (white) people," Big Pig said, taking a long swig from the bamboo water container.

" You mean . . . ."

" Yes, we have walked all the way over from the land of the Ah-meh-li-ka people, and that's a very long walk, Brother."

"You mean, where the skies meet the end of the far land?"

"And then a long piece after you come to the end of the land and the sky." All this had an effect too great for the poor man to bear. It eventually rendered him speechless so that we had to leave him and find the chief's house by ourselves, but he had rushed to the chief by another route and was waiting for us there.

As we entered the village itself, every dog in the vicinity began barking fitfully and converged upon us with snarls and snapping bared teeth. We returned the welcome with well-placed kicks at the dogs and yells to the owners to call them off. Most of the owners simply poked incredulous faces out of the bamboo dwellings and seemed more intent on seeing how many dogs we could dispatch while trying to save our lives. The results were as expected and according to good observance of Lahu laws which say that if a visitor is bitten by village dogs, it is his own damned fault since any reasonable man should be able to kill a dog first. Even the dogs knew this law thoroughly and kept distances just short of the reach of Big Pig's long knife. I had no long knife and the leather in my boots may have attracted the dogs, which led to a very good work out for me in the arts of kicking. The battle ended unbelievably without casualties at the steps of the chief's house.

Every house, about ten in all, had thatchgrass roofing and slatted bamboo walls. They were all new and looked clean enough from a distance. The headman's house was scarcely larger than the other dwellings, but it stood out by the obvious wealth of a single, sad-looking pony which had been tethered under the house. An unassuming little man, face deeply pitted by smallpox scars, invited us to come up the single, notched log which served as the front porch steps. While Big Pig held off the dogs, I walked up the log as quickly as I could and managed it with relief at not having to use my hands, which would have been most undignified. Once on the porch and while entering the house, I lost caution for an instant and ran right into one of the bamboo roof supports. Staggering backwards, I slipped on some discarded vegetables and banana peels, spun round and ran a leg down through the slat flooring. It was disappointing and spoiled the dignity which I had tried so hard to maintain. After all, who wants to entertain guests who are so clumsy and who can't stay on their two feet?

"Ah Chief, your house has no ladder, so the spirits caused your guest to break a slat instead. May good fortune be with you!" I thought of that as I recovered my sunken leg.

" Great, great blessings come today!" he said, looking terribly pleased. My little accident had suddenly taken on a good purpose, being interpreted as the breaking of the ladder rung by a guest which is considered very good luck for the house.

The chief led me into the dark interior of his smoke-filled house and I groped my way in after him. When I had found a spot to squat down by the hearth and had accustomed my eyes to the darkness, I noticed a man lying down to my left smoking opium. It was the second head-man and he was not to be bothered for the moment. I watched him for a while as he toasted the small balls of opium over the flickering flame from an earthen bowl filled with bear fat. To this he periodically touched the bowl of his pipe and drew in the opium smoke deeply, groaning contentment as the smoke slowly spewed from his nostrils.

" I have finished my smoke for the mid-day," the chief said, " and my guest may take that mat over there if he likes."

" I am trying to stop smoking opium, Chief," I replied. And because there is no way in Lahu to simply say, " No, thank you " or " Thank you ", I reached quickly for my pipe in case he would insist on my accepting his ultimate in hospitality. He watched me with a strained uncertainty as to what he should say next or offer.

" You speak like the ' Meu Neu ' Lahu and yet my son-in-law says you come from the Ah-meh-li-ka people."

" Do you know about the Ah-meh-li-ka people? " I asked.

" Only from what people say. Is it true? "

" Yes, I come from the Ah-meh-li-ka people and lived a long time with the Lahu-na."

" Never saw Ah-meh-li-ka people before, but they say that the Flying Machines that came over our village had them riding inside trying to jump into other flying machines which had Ja-Pa (Japanese) people in them when the two people were chasing about in a war which seems to have stopped."

" Where were you then, Chief? "

" My people were living up north of here five days' travel," he replied, pointing towards the Burma border. " We never saw any of the outsiders where we were, but all the hills made much talk about a war about the little yellow people of Ja-Pa and the big hook-nosed people of Ah-meh-li-ka and the Meu-pi-la (British)."

By dusk, and several earthen pots of strong black tea later, we had covered such odd subjects as the earth being round (unacceptable to second headman), what made an aeroplane fly (unbelievable to all), the causes of malaria (impossible! it had to be caused by evil spirits), and the probable Lahu population in the United States by the end of the next dry season. The house had begun to fill with returning members of the chief's family and many, many curious villagers. We left the guest talk temporarily in favour of a matter of village law which the chief had to settle. For this, the good chief addressed no one in particular, but just sat staring at a hole in the roof and spoke in brief, beautifully worded sentences.

The point of justice concerned what should be done

with an unthinking young man who had so much as "looked too long at a newly-married young woman" whose husband was then absent from the village. The young woman testified that it had been nothing and the accused denied his guilt of bad intentions. The "long look" had been witnessed by the girl's brother, an unlovable looking character who demanded justice in fines payable to him. It took the chief about five minutes to stare at the roof and proclaim judgement. "The accused must make it right with the insulted by giving him one chicken of killable size. But according to the law of this land, the chief's wise decision must be repaid by the one who orders justice. And so, Brother of the girl, you must pay me one 'ka' of opium!" This amounted to the price of five chickens. Only Brother John did not snicker with amusement. And now that the "insulted" girl had thus been made more noticeable than ever, and because she was an attractive lass, the jealous brother should have tried to collect a chicken each from all of the men present. He had, however, learned that the price for opium is higher than the price for chickens.

Outside, the sounds so typical of a Lahu village preparing for the night could be heard. Some of the families were doing their rice-pounding before retiring instead of making this an early morning chore. The foot-treaded pounders made rhythmic clunking and thudding noises from several points around the village. Roosters crowed from roosts and pigs squealed noisily as they were being herded into tight pens to secure them from prowling leopards. Somebody had tied up a pup somewhere, and it added persistent mournful yelps to the din of small children's voices coming from the dusty centre of the village. Mothers wailed for disobedient children to come home, and someone wanted to know where in the devil her skinny sow with the four teats and three babies had wandered off to. Everybody and everything in that close community could hear everybody and everything. There were no secrets that would keep for long. If Ca Hkeh beats his wife; or Na Shaw quarrels with her mother-in-law; or Eh-Pa returned the lovesong of E-Sheh: then everybody, including little Hka Co, would be commenting on the event. So it was that one young lad, just married, informed me that he had only popped in to have a quick look at me before returning to his honeymoon which was being conducted far from the village in the jungles. He wanted to tarry longer and listen to all the talk, but as it was getting dark, he must hurry back to his love who had been left on the trail on which tigers walked. If she became frightened, she might run back to her mother which would be sad indeed.

With darkness, chaos seemed to settle down to just the droning of voices from the different houses and the crying of babies. Occasionally, the pony under the chief's house began a vigorous rubbing against the post, causing the whole place to shudder and develop alarmingly into oscillations which one could not be sure would not eventually collapse the frail building. During one of these shudders, I passed the word to Stud Bull that after the visit we would remove ourselves from the village and spend the night under the stars just outside the village. There a man might find some sleep, free from the lice of chickens, dogs and pigs, shuddering houses, crying babies, and the perpetual smoke that hung heavily inside a Lahu dwelling.

The " Paw Khu " or religious headman did not arrive until dinner was about to be served. He came into the chief's house announcing himself in a loud, booming voice and attired in full tribal dress, complete with the red, black and white leggings. There was a wealth of silver ornaments fastened to his jacket and the turban had been done up into an enormous " doughnut " which rode high on his head. He was the picture of good cheer and a big man for a Lahu. I was struck at once by the huge hands, tough and horny from hard blacksmithing. The way was respectfully cleared for him and as he found a place just beside me, he gathered up the loose, very low-crotched pants as though it had been a great skirt and sat down. He had not stopped talking since entering the house.

"And all this time they tell me about the flying machine making people and only today do I get to sit down beside one of those real ' Ka-la-hpu ' people. Ah, it is a good day, elders and young people!" He was practically drooling over me and leaned over after a quick inspection of my person to grab my arm as though it were some piece of merchandise on sale.

"Ah!" he exclaimed in genuine joy. " Look at the arms of a ' Ka-la-hpu ' person. How wonderful. Just like the fur on a Gibbon ape's arms! I wish I had fur like that on my arms." Then after stroking my not unusual complement of forearm hairs, he added, "And do the ' Ka-la-hpu ' women have beautiful hairy arms too? "

" Yes," I told him, because an answer to the contrary would have disappointed him terribly. "And Paw Khu, had you noticed that my beard has a reddish glow? "

"Ah!" he exclaimed again when he had lifted the pine faggot to within singeing distance of my face. " It is so, my People, come see!" With that, I was nearly martyred in the cause of proclaiming the excellence of the Ah-meh-li-ka people. My nose, my strangely coloured hair and even the funny hazel eyes all became important to the mob of Lahus in the chief's house. Somebody even commented that my body odour wasn't like that of a Lahu and that, depending upon the way one looked at it, or sniffed at it, it could be said to be more fragrant or more malodorous than that of the Lahus. Two or three people were for me and several others were against me on that issue.

I finally stood up, waved my arms and made a little speech to save myself any further embarrassments. " Lahu People! Settle down quietly and hear me. Let us not waste further time examining my body because we come to you only for a very brief visit and there are too many important things to discuss with the elders!" That got the Paw Hku and the chief both up on their feet.

"Everybody move back out of the way," the chief ordered, "and if you are a female, stay where you're supposed to—outside or away from the elders! Elders, move over here by the hearth so that men can talk together like men should. Now obey your Chief! There's getting to be just too many people in my house and I am getting mad. If you're important, stay, if not, get out!" Everybody remained almost exactly where they had been, but things did become somewhat more orderly.

Fortunately, the Paw Hku was a most energetic yarn-spinner, and from then on, I had the pleasure of listening to his many tales. His knowledge of jungle herb medicines was inexhaustible and apparently very effective, as evidenced by the surprising good health that seemed to prevail in that village. He claimed to be seventy years old although he did not look much over fifty, and attributed his good physical preservation to: not smoking opium; frequent applications of a mixture of bear gall, marrow of wild goat and a certain nut oil to all of the joints; avoiding the drinking of cold water; smoking a tobacco pipe almost constantly, and having, as he put it, "bred" well all of his adult life through the faithful keeping of at least three wives at all times. With those great hands he had strangled a leopard to death, proudly baring his chest and left arm to show me the scars from the leopard's teeth and claws. He was a fine old man and I could have listened to him all night, but the meal which the chief had announced much earlier began arriving.

There was no fuss about the chief's feast. It was served very quickly by several girls that had had ample training in the feeding of hogs and chickens. The only inconvenience was having to move back from the hearth and practically into the laps of the people behind and around me so that some floor space could be made available upon which the different items could be dumped. First, a large, blackened clay pot was placed to rest against the Paw Hku's knee and braced up at the base with two pieces of firewood to keep it from tipping over. Only the chief, the Paw Hku and I were meant to eat at this time. A smaller clay dish was placed at the edge of the hearth containing what might be called a " dip " at cocktail parties, but actually it was a much rarer concoction of mashed spiders (raw) with ginger and chillipeppers. The red grained mountain rice was served on individual banana leaves and slapped into our individual laps with just the right giggle by a large-breasted girl who had difficulty keeping them inside her flimsy blouse. Almost at once, three badly singed and ash-covered cats arrived to take up strategic positions and the signal to begin was announced by the chief. The Paw Hku's hand shot into the black pot, pulled out a chunk of meat and conveyed it uninspected and directly to his mouth. He held the first-sized chunk in his mouth while he reached over with two fingers and scooped up a good portion of the " dip ". I stalled by asking a young man beside me to adjust the pine faggot so that the black smoke would not come into my eyes and to improve the lighting a bit. That was when I noticed that one of the cats had begun eating from my portion of rice. I gave it a gentle tap on the head and shoved it onto somebody's lap behind me.

Then it was my turn to go fishing in the big black pot. My first venture produced a leaf of mustard green which I put on my rice and for which I would have settled, but the chief's sharp eye noticed that I was being too modest. " Meat," he said, " try some meat first." I tried again and produced the whole hand of a Gibbon just long enough to recognise that the fingernails had not been cleaned. I dropped it promptly back into the soup. My next try found something softer and less bony, with at least all of the skin removed. I have no idea whether or not it tasted good. It was no different from eating pure peppers. By the time I had gulped down enough rice to ease the pain and wiped the tears out of my eyes, the Paw Hku was applying finishing touches to the Gibbon hand, smacking his lips noisily.

The meal is mainly to be remembered in terms of the several problems which attended it. First there was the problem of the enthusiastic audience. The spectacle of a " Ka-la-hpu " eating was a marvellous thing to see, so that soon I was being squeezed so close to the hearth that I had to place my leaf of rice upon my knees. Whenever I had freed my arm from one pair of hair-feeling hands, another pair of hands would take over to comment wondrously about it. To my left rear sat a dear old lady who kept dipping her head down low just behind me. This eventually aroused my curiosity to see what she was up to. The next time her head went down, I turned to have a look and found that she had selected the small floorspace between the two of us for purposes of trying to hit the small crack in the bamboo slats with mouthfuls of betel and tobacco juice. She was missing the mark and scoring very well into my rear pants pocket. I glared fiercely at her and received a full-mouthed smile without the teeth to hide the contents behind the gums. I threatened to shift forward some more and she threatened to come even closer. The dipping, glaring and smiling continued and she was convinced that I really cared a great deal for her by my frequent peerings around at her.

Inevitably, the cats finally got out of hand and the Paw Hku himself became aware of this when one tried to contest him for a monkey bone. It might have been an insect as far as he was concerned and not worthy of much thought at all. Without a word, he simply smashed the cat with a blow from his huge hand and crushed its skull.

He then flung the cat out over the heads of the people and it landed on some of the girls crowding the doorway and made them giggle and laugh. The Paw Hku hardly lost a step in the serious business of eating. I thought others might be sharing my consternation and looked around to study the face of the young man who tended the pine faggots. He was still looking at me and smiled admiringly at the odd expression I gave him. He may or may not have noticed the smashing of the cat.

The room was a combination of odours from many unwashed bodies and the hog pen just beneath the floor. From the chief's sleeping quarters to one side, someone was at the opium pipe again and sending forth a more pleasantly aromatic smell which mingled with the pitch-pine smoke. I had been sitting by the chief's hearth for almost three hours and was badly in need of some fresh air. The meal's conclusion came as a great relief and I stood up to announce that I would take my leave of the chief's fine hospitality. And it had been real hospitality, chaotic and barbaric, but genuine and from the depth of the heart. In a few hours we had bridged forever the gap between total strangers and good friends. These were gentlemen in the backwoods Lahu sense of the word and I knew that I would always cherish their acquaintance.

My companions had made camp about a hundred yards above the last house in the village. The air was pure and sweet and a cool breeze swept through the pine trees on the ridge. It was a brilliantly starry night with a bright quarter moon. Stud Bull gave me a hot mug of coffee and we chatted and laughed together for a while about our Red Lahu reception. Before Big Pig and several of the others joined us, I was in my sleeping bag and remembered hearing a leopard coughing across the valley. Then sleep descended upon me in one swift sweep.

At dawn, the chief and Paw Hku were both squatting by our campfire. They wished us good hunting and told

169

us to return in two or three moons to enjoy the feast of the warrior wasps, and, if we could tarry longer, an effort would be made to chase a gaur herd together. It sounded good to me, and I did take him up on it one day, well after the time the wasps had been " harvested ". We were, however, right on schedule for the gaur and the hunt turned out to be a great, good time.

Life in the Lahu village was just stirring to the activities of a new day as I followed Big Pig down the steep trail which would yet lead over many mountains. An hour later, we crossed a clear, rushing stream and found a campfire still smouldering just off the trail on the other side. A cosy bed of ferns had been recently slept in, but the honeymooners had moved away, leaving only two impressions in the piled up ferns to tell a story of mountain lovers who knew something of carefree joy in the midst of nature's great garden.

Two days short of the motor road to our east, we camped in a high valley in the heart of grasslands which had once been the opium fields of Meo tribesmen some fifty years before. Here the trails of returned big game, elephant, gaur and sambar deer, crossed the stream at every few paces. A huge tiger had moved up the stream during the night before, leaving wet pug marks in the sand and mud. I placed my cap over one of the impressions without being able to completely cover it. He was surely the king over this particular realm.

We made camp where gaur and elephant also liked to bed by the stream. Then Big Pig and I went out to make a preliminary reconnaissance of the area. Not far from camp on a long, sloping ridge we spotted a sambar stag moving slowly through the grass on the opposite ridge at about four hundred yards. It was one of those privileged shots as far as I was concerned, since it is rare in the jungled hills to spot big game at more than a hundred yards. A rifleman in jungles has similar frustrations as the sporting car

enthusiast who has not had a chance in a long time to
" open her up " on a good road. I made a clean and well-
calculated shot which I was proud to mention to other
hunters later. Big Pig, the great hunter had never seen a
kill at more than two hundred yards and had had his doubts
that my ·30/06 could do what it was designed to do. We
stripped the deer's tenderloins and best meat and left the
rest for tiger bait.

By the second day, the tiger had not returned to either
of two sambar baits placed on opposite sides of the valley,
but I was determined to make contact with the owner of
the huge pugs. Towards evening, as Big Pig and I prepared to go out to wait over my first sambar again, I
chanced to look up the slope to our right and was most
astonished to see a small boy duck back out of sight behind
a tree. I thought I was seeing things until the boy stuck
his head out again, ·nd then two more small heads
appeared. My companions were as amazed as I was when
they had all seen the boys. We realised that we could not
possibly be close to a village in big game country of this
sort and thought at first that the boys might have tagged
along to a group of hunters who should be camped nearby.
Then I wondered if the boys might be members of the Phi
Tong Luang, the primitive (or retrogressed?) tribe known
as " Spirits of the Yellow Leaf." We beckoned to the boys
and called out softly in Lahu to come down and join us.

After some time, a little voice called out in Lahu—they
were Lahu after all—and demanded to know what we
were doing there. We told them that we were eating sambar meat and if they cared to join us they were welcome.

" What village are you from? " said the same voice.

" From the little old village of Chiengmai. Now come
on down boys because nobody is going to hurt you," I
called, still sure that they must be children of hunters in
the vicinity.

After considerably more coaxing, the boys came down

and walked cautiously up to the edge of our camp. One had a small bamboo basket on his back and the oldest one, who looked about twelve years old, carried a small hunting knife. The basket contained some freshly dug yams and a large bamboo gopher which had been speared through the neck. The boys had no jackets, only some old rags tied around their waist. Their hair had burrs matted in them and they were not the picture of well-washed boys, but they appeared to be in good physical condition. We finally got their full story straightened out as the boys chewed on pieces of sambar meat.

They were three young brothers who had been turned out into the hills by an opium addict father. He had been cruel to them and had not fed or cared for them. For nearly a year, the boys chose to wander around the jungles instead of finding a home in another Lahu community. Their's might have been the typical story behind the beginning of such nomadic jungle people as the so-called " Spirits of the Yellow Leaf." But because they had been mere boys who had survived at least one brutal rainy season in the high hills, their's was a remarkable experience. The oldest boy, who gave his name as " Eh Kao," had led his two younger brothers, aged eleven and nine, through almost daily perils and was responsible for making the right decisions at every turn which brought them all out alive and even in good healthy condition. It is remarkable enough that none of them died from sickness or wild animal attacks; one good bite from the green viper, so common in the hills, could have complicated into gangrene; or they might have contracted pneumonia, especially during the cold rainy nights. But I marvelled most that the boys did not have sores and infections which are difficult to avoid, and a good number of which I could have shown that day despite my medical kit.

At twelve years, Eh Kao had demonstrated a master woodsman's skill for survival in the jungles. He had not thought much of his accomplishments, even though he had the deep admiration of such as Big Pig. The boys had learned a great deal more from necessity than what had been taught them. As Lahu children, they had learned much that they later had to develop upon for actual survival, but this natural basic training would not have been enough for an average man from the city to survive that long in jungles. Eh Kao simply laughed at my many enquiries and said that he and his brothers had had a wonderful time instead. So that was part of their secret of success, *they simply liked living in the jungles.* And yet they had not had the equipment to tend to one small infection which could have turned to serious complications.

As to be expected, Eh Kao had many stories of the close calls that they had had. Small boys, stalking about in the jungles had seen magnificent big game at close quarters— what grown hunters dream of but rarely see.

The boys remained with us that night, sleeping around the camp fire in a huddle upon warm ashes that they had scooped out. They might not have slept as comfortably on an innerspring mattress. The next morning, Eh Kao laid by the fire, head propped on one hand and the minute I woke he said, looking steadily at me, " This one likes this gang, so this one is going to join you even though I can't speak for my brothers."

Eh Kao did indeed tag along with me from that day until six years later. His brothers were left in the care of the Lahu chief of a village in which we spent a night two days later. We came down from the hills to the Fang road after putting Eh Kao in a pair of under shorts that came down to his knees. He had already designated himself as my personal kit-bag carrier and would not let me out of his sight.

We never got the big tiger on the Nam-mak-uen, but the pleasure of bringing up Eh Kao around my home in Chiengmai was rewarding enough. He grew into a fine-looking and strapping lad and became so Thai-ised that he finally married a lovely Khun-muang girl. Today, the once burr-matted hair is beautiful, oiled and fixed in "duck-tails" and he is quite the young-man-about-town. When he finally drifted off, I did not have to wish him luck—Eh Kao always knew what he wanted and how to manage for himself. He had had a good education in survival.

CHAPTER NINE

Beyond the Spirit Gates

N O one from the seventeen households of Cu-sa-tai village had ever seen a white man. So it remained to be seen whether the stranger's visit would prove good or bad. Final conclusions by all concerned was that it was both good and bad.

The Akha chieftain had shown a primitive friendliness when he realised that my party consisted of Lahu—his own second language—and that the foreigner after all was simply a very odd-looking Lahu himself. He had taken us into the dark interior of his house, offered tea, and commenced in very good Lahu to ask many questions. We were only travellers, we explained, who had come a long way over the hills and needed to spend a night out of the rain. "Yes, yes," he had agreed rather nervously, looking out at the roaring rain. But he was quite sure that we must be at least bandits or opium smugglers. In any case, every "outsider"—especially the strange one—was capable of bringing with him a number of evil spirits.

Big Pig had often been through Akha villages, and even spoke a smattering of their language. I was hoping that he could soon set the old gentleman at ease, and that the stopover might give me an opportunity to learn something about the then little-known Akha. Among other things, I had hoped to photograph their interesting dress, especially the women's. Not until some years later did anthropologists really get a good look at the Akha. Before that, sketchy accounts had been written which rather mixed the different tribes together. These people fascinated me because of the numerous accounts that I had heard from the Lahu. Anthropologists still have a long way to go towards a more thorough understanding of the Akha.

We sat in a double-partitioned thatch-roofed house, walled by bamboo slats, with the ground for the floor. There was an entrance at both ends of the roughly twenty by forty foot long dwelling with racks to one side for storage of practically everything that the Akha must keep, rice in bamboo bins, primitive agricultural tools, jars of rice liquor in various stages of fermentation, old skins, bones, yam tubers, birdlime, coils of snares, and a motley assortment of smoke-blackened articles. A more progressive village than this might have a few pack saddles hung from the rafters. I was wondering about finding even a yard-long space a foot wide on which I might try to sleep that night. It looked like the choice might be to sit around the hearth all night.

When the rain had stopped it was nearly dusk, and the people began to drift into the chief's house in alarming numbers, filling the place with smells that made the wildest Lahu home seem like the open woods. Women and girls with their over-decorated headdress and short, very short, skirts that hung precariously low on the hips, stared at us with obvious curiosity. Probably because this was a rather wild and backward village even by Akha standards, the women were not much concerned about modesty as they began hunkering down across from the Lahu men and me. We tried not to notice, but I could see that even New Soul was trying to conceal his embarrassment behind a facade of comical great self-importance. It took Big Pig to get things rearranged.

" Chief of Akha," he said turning to the old man, " when men must sit around the fire and discuss important things, it is difficult to think wisely when women squat about before them."

" Ah, it is so, it is so," Chief agreed, not grasping immediately what Big Pig had been referring to. He finally became aware, probably for the first time, and ordered the women to go away. They left in a bobbing of bare breasts, giggling delightedly that men noticed them. Some of them had, by western standards, a beauty which was camouflaged by the strange attire and because soap was unknown to them.

" How was the harvest last year, Akha Chief? " I asked trying to draw things into a conversational focus.

" Field rats and birds (munias) took most of the crop, but the rats were fat when we caught them, and they were good to eat," he replied, as though it had been an averagely successful year.

I owed much to the fact that New Soul, Gets Lost, Stud Bull, and New Frog all knew how to keep straight faces. Had they laughed or made sly remarks to one another during our stay, the Akha would never have spoken without inhibitions as they did. These were simple folks who had not developed any reserve towards strangers, and assumed their many odd customs to occasion nothing but solid understanding with visitors. Many of their strange ways have never been reported in formal works of ethnology simply because the interviewed realised that the interviewers thought their ways were unusual. This has led to controversies between students of tribal lore.

The conversation soon turned to matters concerning hunting. It turned out that the Akha in that area had taken over old lands which had been previously hunted out by the Lahu. They were reduced to finding small game and an occasional barking deer or wild pig. Thus they had perfected very good methods of trapping and snaring, and more than in the past, learned to eat anything that represented meat, often to the amusement of the other tribes. They raised numbers of pigs and chickens, and the main purpose of the numerous dogs around the village was for meat. Dog meat has been a traditional delicacy for the Akha, being considered superior to goat meat.

"If a man does not get to eat the meat of dogs, his heart does not feel well," the old chief had explained at one point.

Two dripping young boys, soaked from the driving rain, came into the house. One of them had a gourd bowl full of what looked like maggots to me—probably a palatable variety, I guessed. A woman took this from the boys and seemed as pleased as if it had been a fine trout. I never saw what happened to them, nor felt like asking.

"Chief, your village seems like a strong, well-organised place, you must have very complete law and order here," Big Pig said, carefully concealing his strong doubts.

"We manage well," the chief replied. "We have the chief, two second chiefs, and wise elders. We have our own religious leader, but at the times for making women of the virgins, we call for the village ' male ' from another place."

"It is better to call the *aw-shaw* from another place anyway," Big Pig replied knowingly and with a quick wink at me.

"We do not have many girls to prepare each season for marriage," the chief continued, "because many of the daughters disobey proper Akha laws and run away with the boys who come to steal them from other villages. Ah, the young people cause much grief to the old people these days."

The old Akha custom required that girls had to first become properly eligible for marriage by going through a special ceremony in which they were devirginised by the chosen "male." This was believed to insure fertility and protect against the bad spirits which would harm health and prolificacy. The deflowering ceremony, as it is known to all non-Akha observers, probably began to die out from Akha customs as the formerly large village groups broke up into what are today relatively smaller ones and which are simply hamlets in many cases. In such situations as this, it became more commonplace for a young man to simply " steal " a young wife from some distant village or hamlet. The ceremony is certainly no longer widely practised and witnessed by no one except the Akha themselves. In most cases, Akha men will never discuss this very private ritual with any outsider. The chief of the Cu-sa-tai Akha, however, had not thought it out of the ordinary to mention the subject, boasting that he had himself been an *" aw shaw "* or " male " at one time. This was like admitting that he had been the pastor of the village church; for the ritual is a solemn and holy thing with the Akha.

The elaborate " spirit gate " that we had passed through on the way up the ridge to the village had aroused considerable interest on my part. We had come at a time when the Akha had recently concluded some sort of religious ceremony and a freshly slaughtered dog, its skin stretched out between bamboos with the head still attached, had been hanging from the cross piece over the top. The whole gate, consisting of two pillars crossed at the top by a beam, was a jumble of many woven spirit symbols, some to ward off the evil ones and others to attract the good ones. At the base of the pillars were wooden carvings, crudely made, representing human copulation—symbols which were believed to retain fertility within the village. " The gate is made beautiful for the good spirits and ugly for the evil spirits," the chief had explained.

I was just beginning to learn something about the Akha and their curious customs when a commotion in the other section of the chief's house suddenly became more intensified, with people coming in and out and jabbering loudly in a tongue that we did not understand. I assumed that all of the women the chief had ordered away earlier had simply gathered there and had become involved in some quarrel. A young man came up to the chief and said something rapidly to him in a low voice. The chief got up angrily and barged through the crowd into the other room.

In a little while he was back again and told me very gruffly to come with him into the other room. I went with him, pushing my way with great difficulty through the numerous Akha crowded around a young girl lying on a mat and propped up by a man. She appeared to be dead.

For a few moments, I watched a wizened old man who had just arrived, begin his various spirit incantations. He shook various charms and what looked like rattles over the girl, muttering all the while in his guttural "spirit talk" and going through several stanzas of a wailing song-like chant. The man holding the girl would periodically put his finger on the patient's glazing eyes and when there was no reaction, began yelling angrily. The girl had apparently been lying there for quite a long time before we arrived, and I took it that her illness had not come on suddenly.

"There," the chief said furiously to me, "an Akha girl dies!"

"What causes her to die?" I asked, trying to appear calm.

"Not every day Akha women die," he replied, suddenly shouting. "*You* come into our village, and a girl dies! Why do you do this to us? *You* brought the evil spirits, now *you* bring her back!"

I was appalled. To him it was obviously that simple and he really believed that. The stern faces all around me showed no hint of understanding or sympathy that an "outsider" was being wrongly accused of such a terrible thing. I knew at once that I could not be any more misunderstood, no matter what I did, so I decided to go forward to the girl and tell the man who was holding her to at least stop his yelling and refrain from jabbing the girl's eyes with his filthy fingers. I asked them to loosen the tight cords that held the girl's headdress and which seemed to be choking her. This was immediately refused, and probably interpreted as a further design on my part to hasten death with a final " disgracing " act, since the women's headdress can not be removed in the presence of men. I felt her pulse, causing even a greater din of protests, and found that the girl was just about gone.

" Chief, you must believe me that I do not cause this girl to die," I said, standing up again and shouting at the top of my voice. " If I could help, I would do everything that I could." He just looked at me with a horrible expression of insane hate.

I saw someone pointing to his lower abdomen, apparently explaining that the spirit had taken hold there. This I took to mean that the girl had complained of a pain there before losing consciousness. Though I will never be certain of it, the girl probably died of a ruptured appendix.

The chief spoke again, this time mostly in Akha, and continued his terrible accusations. It made no difference that the girl had been sick for days before our arrival. I gave up any further attempts to explain, and feeling thoroughly frightened at the prospects of being mobbed, shoved my way out into the other room as quickly and with as much dignity as I could muster. My Lahu men had already found out what was happening and seemed to realise at once how serious the situation had become. Big Pig informed me that men were running back to their various houses for their weapons. He told me quickly that our only chance was in pulling a careful bluff.

The whole thing had come on so suddenly that I was unable to think clearly. Stud Bull looked very worried as he handed me my revolver. Big Pig, always cool and steady anywhere else, had for once, an uneasiness which served to further intensify my own fears. " What do we do now? " I asked him, feeling quite helpless. Big Pig whispered rapid instructions into my ear as the Akha chief started up again in a new wailing and began pointing his finger at me. I got Big Pig's message and stood up, probably without a minute more to lose.

" Akha Chief and all men! " I shouted as loudly as I could. " Listen carefully to words that will mean the life or death of every one of you! Your intentions are evil, so I call upon my ten thousand guardian spirits to kill you all, every one, even the chickens, pigs and dogs! " I paused from this fantastic tirade and noticed that the din of voices had suddenly subsided. It was a desperate course of negotiation that I had to push and make good.

A brief silence followed, then I saw the muzzle of a gun being worked through the bamboo slats from the outside. At this point, I yelled right into the chief's face. " Command your people to drop their guns immediately or I call the spirits this moment! "

With eyes fairly popping out of his head, the old boy reacted with a single command that probably prevented certain disaster at the very last moment. It was still not over. I had yet to press my bluff until all chances of a sneaked attack were over. I continued with my ridiculous claim, making a great show of raising my hands and pretending to communicate with unseen things above. For a few moments there I knew something of what it was like to be a witchdoctor, and marvelled at myself that when I was really frightened enough I could put on a pretty good show.

" What will it be, Chief, do we see whose guardian spirits are the more powerful or shall I tell my ten thousand spirits to wait? " I asked, hands still raised.

" Please have mercy on the Akha people! " the chief replied, suddenly changing from his former rage to pitiful meekness. I felt awful—like some miserable, cruel bastard of a cad. But there had been no other recourse except death that night. I took no delight whatsoever in the poor Akha's belief that I could summon greater spiritual help than they could themselves. Yet I had to address them in the only terms they knew.

" I have made a deal with my guardian *nye*," I told the chief and for the benefit of some twenty armed Akha outside. " If anyone turns against his word and lays a hand on me or on any of my men, the *nye* will deal most drastically with the rest of the village as well as with that man. But if you are people of honourable words and intentions, you will be well blessed."

It all came to a peaceful end. We were not even required to find a wet camp outside in the bush that night, moving instead to another Akha house. Once settled there, I felt very depressed about the whole thing and thought how sad it had been that nothing could have been done for the poor girl. To make matters worse, the Akha still believed that I had caused the girl's death because it had been my whim and because I could get away with it with so many guardian spirits at beck and call. They now sought my approval for anything they had to do concerning the dead girl. The chief had come to me to ask if it was all right to fire off guns, above and below the village, in the custom of the Akha for " sending the soul of a dead person." I consented sadly and wanted to weep for these poor, ignorant folk. Death, to them, was always caused by the evil spirits except in the case of old age. It was hopeless to explain to them in the simplest of scientific terms what caused illnesses. In the morning, they would have to add more fixtures to the spirit gates and the witchdoctor would have to spend a great deal of time and energy " chasing " away the particular evil spirits which had come into the village as free riders on the backs of visitors. I knew that such reasons as this had been among the great motivations borne by my forebears who tried to show such primitive people a better way of life and above all, a freedom from fear of the imagined presence of " evil spirits."

I was thoroughly purged that night for deceiving the Akha. The punishment came in the form of countless fleas, ants and bedbugs which cared not in the least that the foreign visitor was supposed to be powerfully guarded by helpful spirits. It was a sleepless night, disturbing enough without the insect invaders. Even New Soul's tough hide did not protect him and many were the eloquent invectives that came from his end of the narrow platform upon which we all huddled. What was enough to make New Soul complain was really more than the rest of us could bear. I chose to sit with Big Pig for most of the night near the fire.

The dawn was a most welcome event and we left without a thought of trying to get pictures of the Akha. I had to wait for years until an Akha village nearer to the town of Chiengrai became understanding enough to allow photography. For good reasons, I chose never to sleep again in an Akha village, preferring even some dusty spot where the pigs rooted on the outskirts of a village to another exposure to the voracious host within Akha dwellings.

We walked past the spirit gates and paused to look at the gruesome mess of a newly slaughtered dog that had been placed there. The row of three separate gates, with the newest one at the outermost point, stood in ominous silence broken only by the buzzing of several large wasps working determinedly at the pieces of flesh which were still attached to the dog skin. Something about this mute spectacle said, " Go, and do not return! "

Big Pig frowned, still gazing at the gates, then began to speak in a loud voice, surprising all of us and drawing our attention. He spoke with mock formality, yet there was something about his little speech that informed us all that he had good reason for this bit of showmanship.

" Oh gates," he began, " stand silently and sturdily. Guard the Akha people from all harm and dangers. Do not let the mere eating up of your legs by the termites of the soil turn your attention away from your duties. Whenever travellers come again, remove the bad spirits from them and cause them to become confused in the meshes of woven things and pierced by the sharp things amongst your members." Then as an afterthought he added, " And wish those who travel away and beyond your guarding arms good fortune while you let the evil spirits ride away with them. Take one last look at these people who come from a faraway place and do not be concerned that you will see them again! Rest easy, gates, and rest easy, Akha people!"

We all sensed that Big Pig wanted the rest of us to keep silent and to follow him down the long ridgeline. He indicated this with a simple toss of his head when he had finished speaking. When we had reached a turn in the trail some hundred yards down the hill, he turned to me and asked, " Did you see them? "

." No," I replied, puzzled.

" And the rest of you, with eyes as big as teacups? " Big Pig asked the other Lahu in our group. Each one admitted that he had not seen " them " whoever they were.

Big Pig shook his head sadly. " Trust the big eyes of other people and the Big Pig wouldn't be around much longer. On the left side of the trail below the gates was something any man calling himself a hunter should have seen. There were enough Akhas there, armed, to shoot up the whole bunch of us! "

Now the reason for his little speech at the gates was clear enough. Big Pig had spotted them at once and noticing that the men were simply waiting to see if we would do some sacrilege to the gates, he had not given out any alarm. He explained that had the Akha looked like they would actually ambush us, he would have let us know soon enough. And had any one of us tried to get too near the gates, he would also have stopped us, thus letting the Akha know that we were going on our way peacefully, to leave them and their gates unharmed. The speech of " blessing " had been for the benefit of those that waited.

It had actually been another very close call. The slightest thoughtless act by any one of us could have been immediately taken by the Akha to mean that we had defiled their holy place. New Soul admitted later that in his personal disdain for the spirit gates, he had felt like tossing the small stick in his hand at the carved figures. It would have been the merest of momentary whims—a reflex—but possibly enough to have angered the waiting Akha.

This visit with the Akha of Cu-sa-tai had been the only time when misunderstandings led to a close shave with any of the hill people of northern Thailand in my entire experience. It had been the sort of thing that might have been possible anywhere among primitive people, but I had always been most fortunate with the tribes that I met in other places. With few exceptions, they have always shown the friendliest hospitality and were most understanding when we at times violated their customs in small ways through our unwitting acts or speech.

As far as I was to be concerned, passing the Akha spirit gates that morning marked a day after which events were to change. It was one of the last days spent with a unit of my original Lahu companions. Since that trip, I could not find opportunity to join the Lahu on any extended trip of any kind, and perhaps because by then I had accomplished most of my ambitions towards the things that a Lahu hunter normally sets out to do, my motivations for hunting changed as well. To me, it is significant that not a single important big game trophy was added to my collection since that day. We all seemed, for various reasons of our own, to have come to our individual forks in the trail about which Big Pig had something to say when we first met.

The last evening we spent in the quiet hospitality of a Yao headman's house, While the rest of the boys chatted gaily with a group of young Yao girls, Big Pig and I sat drinking tea and brooding over the news I had given him about change that was soon coming concerning my own occupational activities. We both knew that our merry roaming together in the hills was drawing to a close and the feeling was of mutual reluctance to see the day come.

"Jaw Maw, before we came to this day the trails were sometimes hard on the feet, but it never failed to make the heart feel happy. Maybe we should never have come to the Akha gates."

I could not answer him immediately, although he had expressed in his own figurative way just what I had been thinking.

"Brother," I replied finally, "I have known you to be wrong only once—when you predicted my fourth daughter to be a boy!"

Big Pig pulled out his skinning knife, inspected the blade briefly and casually cut off a wart from just below his kneecap. Then he pressed the tip of the blade tightly to the spot to arrest the flow of blood. Holding the knife in this position, he seemed to have forgotten his little personal surgery as quickly as he had decided to do it.

"No, I wasn't really wrong about that. You deceived me by not telling me accurately about important rituals you did or did not observe when your daughter was conceived," he replied without looking again at the knife on his knee. He laughed again as he had laughed that morning when I had returned from the Chiengmai hospital, happily amazed over the birth of my fourth daughter. Big Pig had been so sure that it would be a boy that he had come down from his village to take his due credit for proper prediction. I smiled back at him, thinking that I had been spending too much time away from my family.

I thought back over our long and happy association together. We had stepped over many a fallen log and ducked under many jungle obstructions together. There had been many a mark on the soft sides of jungled mountains where one or the other of us had blazed a foothold and into which the other had stepped. It is such recollections that are most vivid to me. They will remain inscribed in my memory as long as I live even though they originate from the briefest glimpses.

We had become a part of the great forests in which we roamed, registering our tracks and signs with those of the wild creatures. For me, as well as the Lahu, it had been the thrill of this sort of association more than anything else that compelled us to return to a particular area or to search out new places. Certainly, the hunting of big game was of secondary importance to the greater desire that we had to be associated together within a setting that we mutually loved. To the Lahu, hunting instincts have been encouraged and developed since childhood. It was not much different in my case since I had been raised with them as a child. But as strong as these motivations had been, we had not taken up the hunt only because of the early training to simply go out and hunt. Nor was it because we, like any hunter, have basic fondnesses for guns and for shooting; this could be satisfied much more conveniently and thoroughly on a shooting range. There are much more deeply-rooted reasons—more important reasons—which concerned not only the desire to be in the forest but also the fellowship of men sharing the things of mutual interest. For my own part, I was primarily concerned with learning something not only of the forest but of the hill people themselves. While learning these many lessons, I could attempt to walk similar trails and experience some of the problems that early pioneers and woodsmen knew; thus it became possible to appreciate with better understanding history itself. I had, in addition, an opportunity to learn something about myself.

The thrill of the chase for some great beast, or the overwhelming feeling attending those moments when tables were turned and the animal came crashing down upon the hunter, were only brief periods of the time spent. For me, these experiences are unforgettable because through them I came to know something more of the nature of the great beasts concerned. I think of gaur and elephant not as huge, ponderous animals, but as agile, incredibly powerful and alert creatures which have a fantastic ability to remain unseen despite their large body masses. I think of tiger and leopard not as voracious predators, but as superbly intelligent hunters that travel long distances and know the meaning of hunger as well as the comfort of a full stomach. Then there are the brutish-appearing wild pigs which to me are only deceivingly so, for beneath their facade of stupidity is tremendous speed, power, and quick deduction. And the bear, not in any way the last or the least of the " big six " which at times can take the best hunter away, might seem clumsy and slow, but hidden in his outward apearance are keen senses, clever judgement, and an admirable ability to use his strength when and where he must have it. There is a respect and admiration for the " dangerous " ones which comes only from having followed them on the hunt. When a man challenges an animal he sees something of the intelligence and courage that is otherwise a mystery hidden deep in the forest.

Yet the potentially dangerous game which challenge hunters are only a small fraction of the jungle's great treasury. Of what the hunter might call game or non-game among the large and small animals alike, there are many and varied lessons to be learned. It would require yet another and fuller volume to describe the reptiles, mammals, and birds which have arrested my attention most on the majority of my time spent in the jungle. These I did not hunt except for scientific purposes, and because they surrounded me wherever I stopped, there were times for simply looking and listening.

Here were the sights and sounds to occupy a man's time completely, from the simplest insect activities to the graceful sambar stag rubbing his horns against a sapling. The sounds of the jungles alone would be enough to cause me to go again to the many places visited. Having had the pleasure to associate various wildlife sounds with the great forests, the lone call of some small owl in the middle of a city seems at once out of place, yet it is a most welcome sound which brings back many memories of the kind of places where the particular species of owl normally lives. As for me, my appreciation for beautiful music from some orchestra, great as it is, does not surpass that which comes from the jungle's many voices. While the different instruments which make up an orchestra can be identified easily enough, this particular pleasure never ends, nor can all sounds always be identified when listening to the sounds of wild creatures. Here the new or unfamiliar sound can always be expected to thrill the listener and to make him wonder about what the source might be or look like. Familiar sounds never pall; instead they stir the senses refreshingly, especially when they have been missed for a long time.

It is a certainty that there are few places in the world today where the tide of civilisation moves so rapidly, while the remote wilderness may still enjoy its unique ways. For Thailand, "The Land of the Free," this uniqueness is one among many splendours which crown this happy kingdom. Although the people of the hills must eventually come into step with civilisation's ways, the process is coming to them in gentle steps through an understanding government. This is a far cry from the turmoil which has surrounded the simple jungle folk in countries which adjoin Thailand. And with this inevitable change, the mountain people will not have lost their unique standing, but rather they will be gaining a stature of which they can be proud. This future is a bright one, although it would be foolish to say that there might not be a few growing pains for the people of the hills. Thailand's determination to become a highly developed nation is no less intense than her desire to preserve the national heritages, including her forests and the colourful tribal groups. With this have come wildlife and forest laws; and step by step, education and welfare for the remote peoples to bring them closer to the rest of the nation.

I went to the jungles, and I hope I shall always have opportunities to go again to look and listen and sometimes to follow the track of big game. This in itself was reward enough, but people who live in and near the jungle, such as the Lahu, gave me entirely new perspectives and reasons to love this sort of adventure. The greatest of my pleasures is in having had the chance to share with such people a life that was uncomplicated yet intensely educational, meagre in the basic necessities yet most healthful, and which had as its standard the love and respect for fellow man and the wild creatures of the forest. Here the balance of nature alone really controls, with the unending cycles of events for man as well as beast, and far away, beyond the massive mountain escarpments, cities boom in an entirely different existence.

NORTHERN THAILAND

Author's Routes:

Walking - - - - -

By Jeep ~~~~

Camps ●1

Scale:

1 inch = approx. 50 Kms

N

BURMA

●4

●5

●6

●7

●8

⊙ Chieng

● MAEHONG SORN

⊙ Pai

⊙ Khun Yuam

●10

●9

● CHIEN

● LAMP

●13

●11

⊙ Mae Sarieng

Hawt ⊙

●12

Ping River

Wang